FOOTBALL ACCESS

Richard Saul Wurman

Armament 2
Weights & Measures 10
Injuries 12
Playing Field 14
Time Factors 16
Terms 18
Officials 20
Rules & Penalties 22
Plays & Formations 24
TV Viewing 38
Stadia 40
Salaries 42
Coaches 44
History of College Football 47
History of Professional Football 50
Collegiate Football Records 54
Professional Football Records 62
Bowl Games 68
Superbowl 70
Player Positions 72

Armament

Only astronauts are packed into as much gear as *Footballus Americanus.*

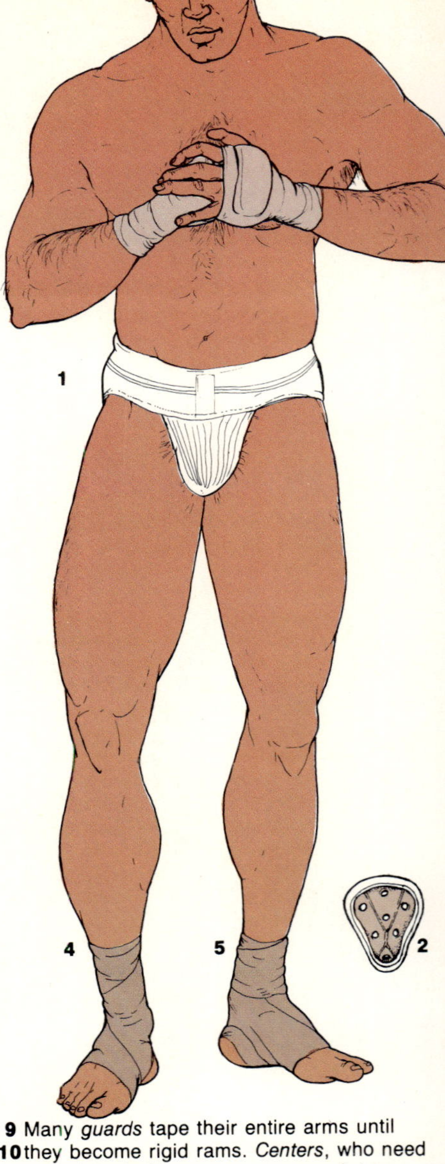

Fully armored for combat, a 270-pound lineman is clad in 14 to 18 pieces of hard and soft equipment. The average weight of all this laboratory-engineered protection: about 13 pounds. Padding of 30 years ago is far bulkier, up to 20-25 pounds per man. But the *Synthetic Era* has taken a large load off players' backs.

"A man picks up an added 3 to 4 pounds of sweat in a game," report NFL equipment chiefs, **"so the coming of foam products, nylon, urethane, vinyl and other lightweight materials is a blessing."**

Equipage, the order in which players get dressed, and average cost of armor:

First to be donned are boxer-type shorts of scrotal-support design, over which goes a
1 polyester **jockstrap** and (sometimes) over
2 that a foam-rubber **protective cup.** A heavy elastic back-abdomen supporter can be added. *Cost: $35.*

3 Next come a cotton **T-shirt** and thick,
4 ribbed, elastic-banded **socks.** *Cost: $15.50*

Taping (the vital element) and wrapping follows. As much as *125 miles* of elastic tape is needed per season by one squad. The NFL is rated the *single largest elastic tape user in the world.* Up to 10 yards of tape may be used in wrapping 2 ankles. Ankles get particular attention. This is a 4-part process. Few players shave their legs anymore (wives and girl friends don't like it). Two to 3 trainers begin with a quick-dry spray *undercoat* which relieves itching. Then Teflon® heel-and-lace pads go over the
5 instep and ankle. Light, rubbery **Pro Wrap** comes next, followed by the tape itself. Shoes are taped to feet and ankles in most cases to prevent sprains.

First taping is finished 20-25 minutes before the kickoff, taking care of ankles and knees. After the players return from pre-game warmup, trainers go to work on hands, shoulders, elbows, etc.

Hands, wrists, arms: Fingers get jammed, so often are taped together, except for
6 *offensive linemen* who tape just their
7 thumbs. *Running backs* tape wrists and forearms to a point below the elbow.
8 *Wide receivers* and *defensive backs* tape their forearms, since a certain amount of stickiness exists and aids in pass-catching. (Pure *stickum* has been outlawed.)

9 Many *guards* tape their entire arms until
10 they become rigid rams. *Centers,* who need to feel the ball on snaps, use much less wrap of the *bubble* (packing material)
11 type. *Quarterbacks* use the least tape of all, for body freedom, with just the wrists and ankles wrapped.

Knees account for 25 per cent or more of serious lost-time injuries, so they get the heaviest wrapping.

Legs are taped from the ankle to the belly
12 of the calf. Elastic **ankle braces** are sometimes worn under the tape to help prevent sprains.

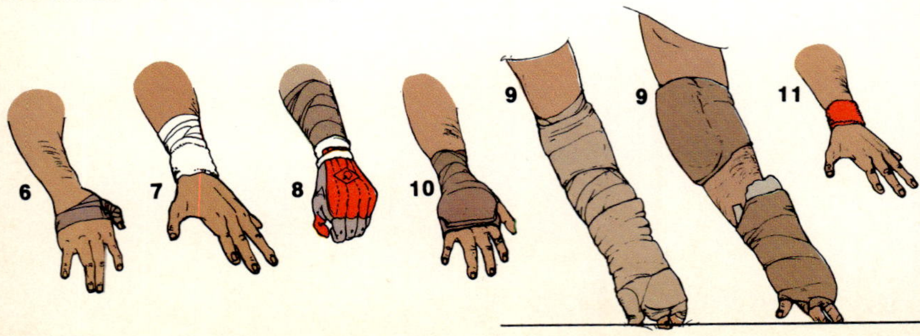

Armament

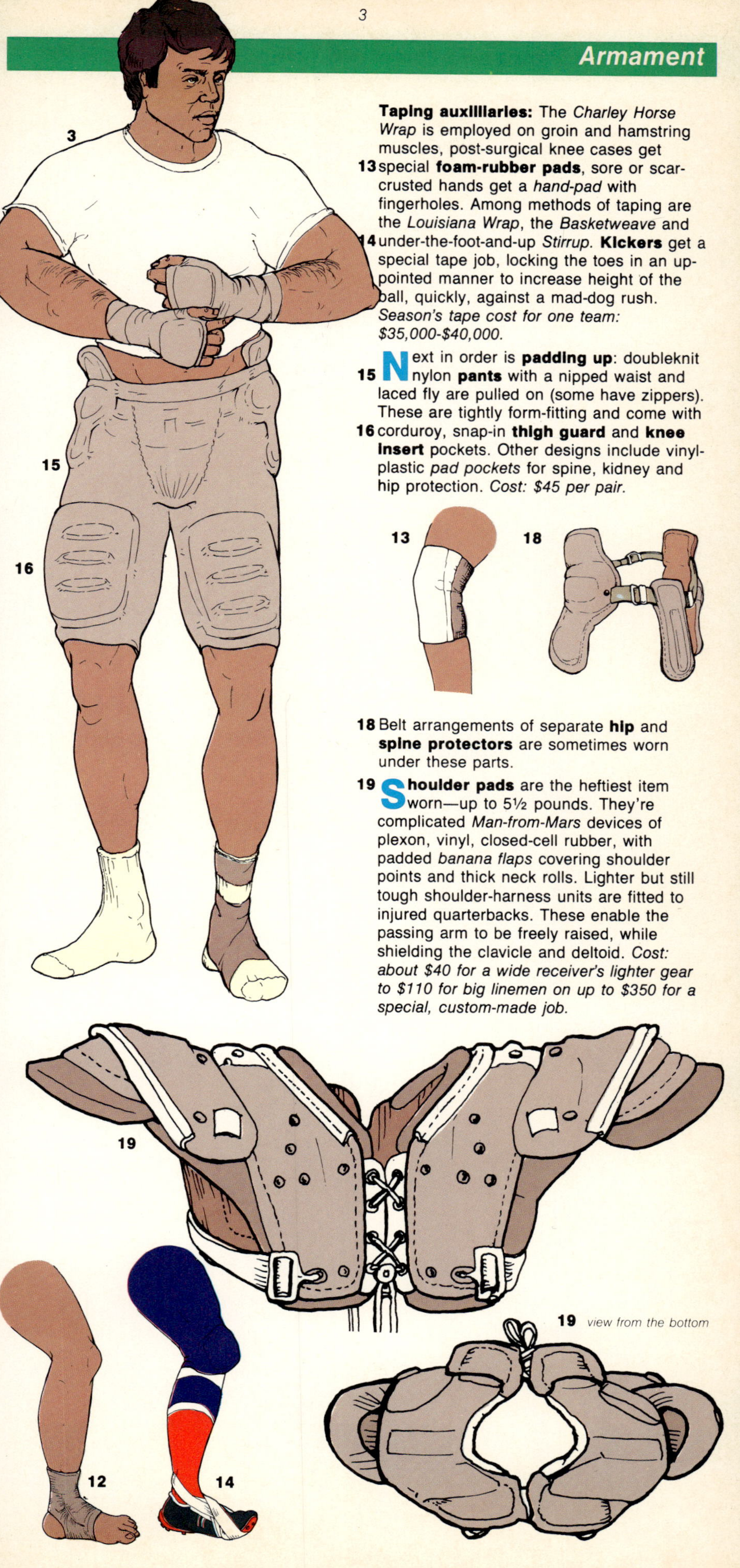

Taping auxilliaries: The *Charley Horse Wrap* is employed on groin and hamstring muscles, post-surgical knee cases get
13 special **foam-rubber pads**, sore or scar-crusted hands get a *hand-pad* with fingerholes. Among methods of taping are the *Louisiana Wrap*, the *Basketweave* and
14 under-the-foot-and-up *Stirrup.* **Kickers** get a special tape job, locking the toes in an up-pointed manner to increase height of the ball, quickly, against a mad-dog rush. *Season's tape cost for one team: $35,000-$40,000.*

15 **N**ext in order is **padding up**: doubleknit nylon **pants** with a nipped waist and laced fly are pulled on (some have zippers). These are tightly form-fitting and come with
16 corduroy, snap-in **thigh guard** and **knee insert** pockets. Other designs include vinyl-plastic *pad pockets* for spine, kidney and hip protection. *Cost: $45 per pair.*

18 Belt arrangements of separate **hip** and **spine protectors** are sometimes worn under these parts.

19 **Shoulder pads** are the heftiest item worn—up to 5½ pounds. They're complicated *Man-from-Mars* devices of plexon, vinyl, closed-cell rubber, with padded *banana flaps* covering shoulder points and thick neck rolls. Lighter but still tough shoulder-harness units are fitted to injured quarterbacks. These enable the passing arm to be freely raised, while shielding the clavicle and deltoid. *Cost: about $40 for a wide receiver's lighter gear to $110 for big linemen on up to $350 for a special, custom-made job.*

Armament

1 **Other shields: thumb-knuckle
protectors** resembling a boxer's glove
cut off at the fingers; *derotation braces* for
the knee, lessening impact of a tackle-hit from
2 the side; spiral-springed **knee cartilage**
3 **shock absorbers; knee-action stabilizers**
4 with hinged steel braces; pliable **elbow**
5 **braces; biceps pads;** snap-on
6 **wrist braces** of padded cotton; *thigh-cap
sponges* under which hot or cold healing
packs may be worn during games;
7 soccer-type **shinguards** worn under the
socks; *cellophane plastic wrap* next to the
skin on very cold days, said to have been
pioneered by the Philadelphia Eagles. *Cost
for each item ranges from $4.50 to $45.*

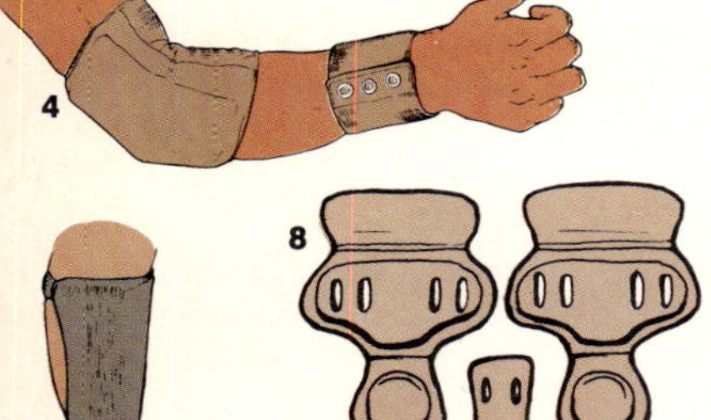

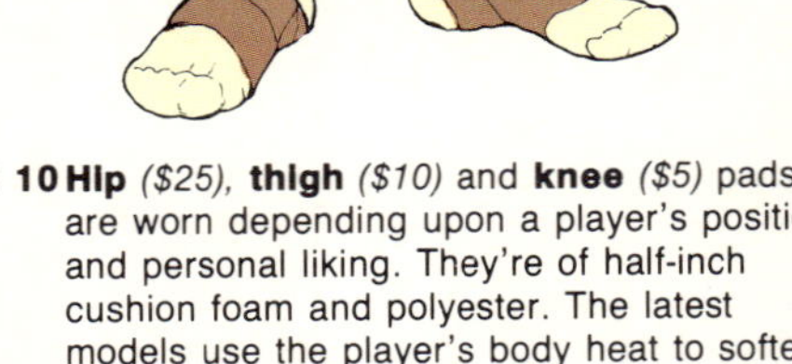

8 9 10 Hip *($25)*, **thigh** *($10)* and **knee** *($5)* pads are worn depending upon a player's position and personal liking. They're of half-inch cushion foam and polyester. The latest models use the player's body heat to soften and mold pads to his particular contours.

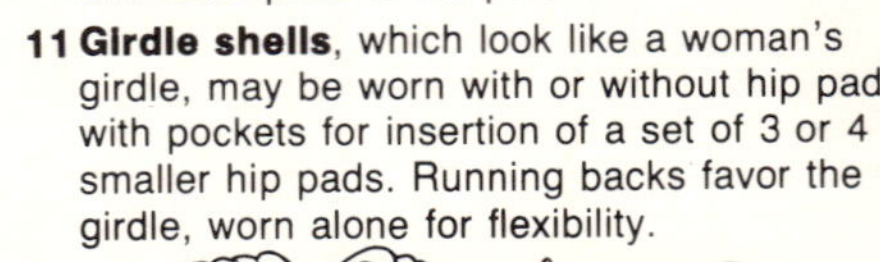

11 Girdle shells, which look like a woman's girdle, may be worn with or without hip pads with pockets for insertion of a set of 3 or 4 smaller hip pads. Running backs favor the girdle, worn alone for flexibility.

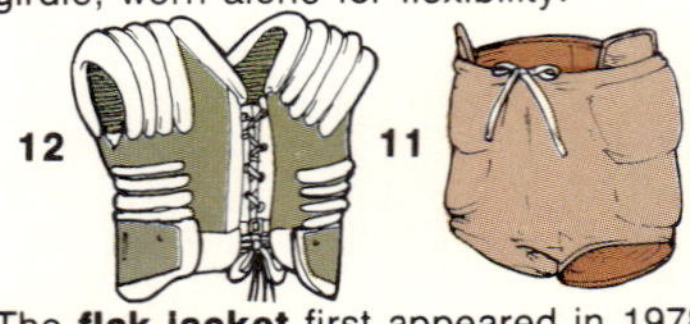

12 The **flak jacket** first appeared in 1978. It was the product of inventor **Byron Donzis**, now one of the most talked-about furnishers of gridiron armor. The Donzis jacket weighed only 7 ounces and was an inflated vest first designed to protect the broken ribs of Houston quarterback **Dan Pastorini.** Other QBs soon copied. The vest's air pockets absorbed a blow so well that the maimed and aching could continue playing.

13 *Cost: $310.* Donzis' new **Rib Protector** is being used extensively by pro and Pop Warner teams alike, and has virtually replaced the original flak jacket.

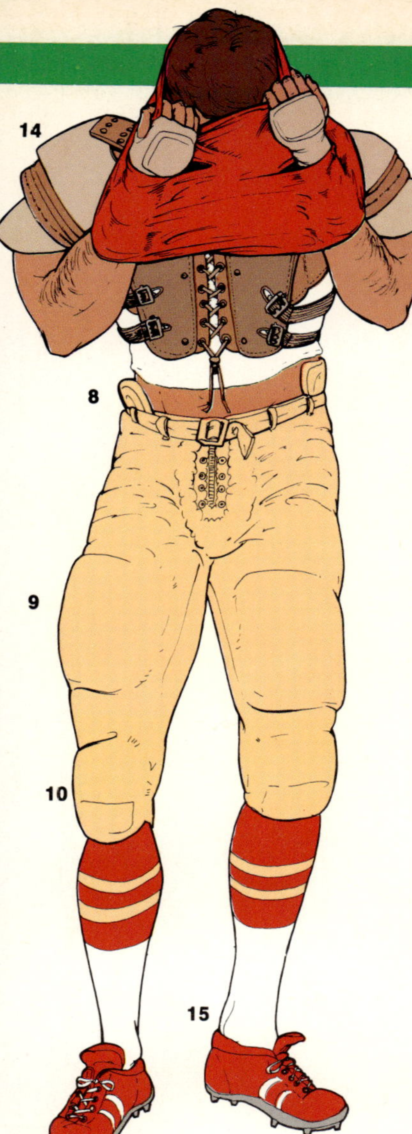

shoes of the 20s

Shoes of today are a far cry from the
clumsy hightops of yesterday with their
16 metal cleats. **Grass shoes** (used on natural
turf) have 7 rubberized cleats, 5 in front and
2 behind, which screw into posts which are
17 shielded to prevent cuts. **Artificial-turf
shoes** have 30 to 100 cleats, shorter cleats
than grass shoes, distributed over molded
18 soles. Then there are **Canadian broomball**
shoes, handy on a soft field, which have 15
to 20 suction cups on the soles. When
stadia switch from synthetic to grass turf, it
causes many footgear problems. In the case
of the Orange Bowl in Miami, which
switched to real grass in 1976, the change
caused visiting teams to use 7 different
types of shoes in one season.

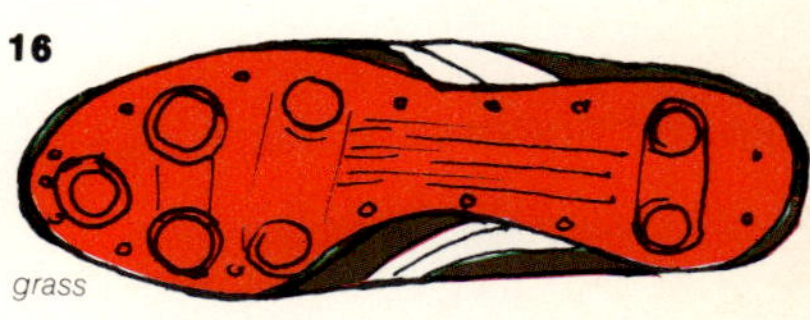

grass

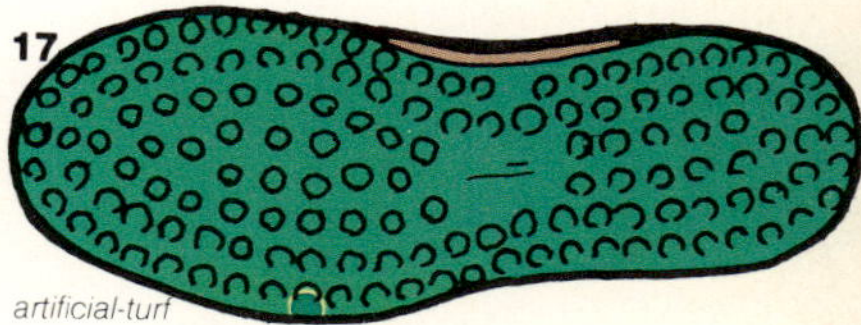

artificial-turf

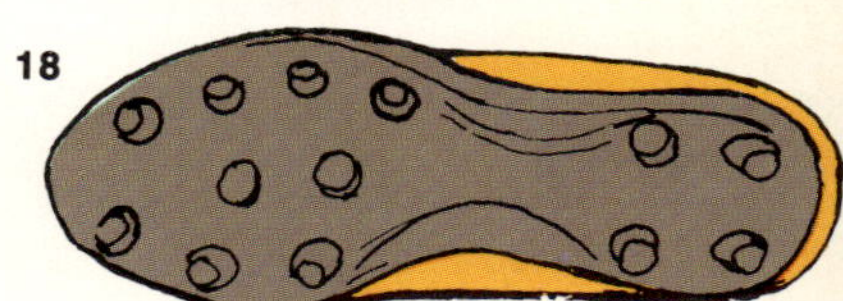

Canadian Broomball

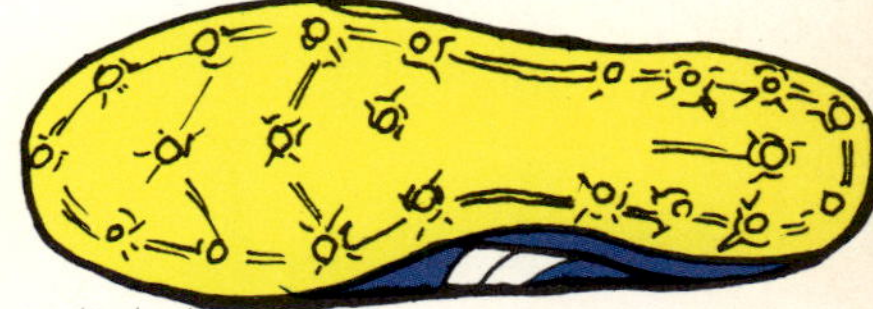
running back

kicking

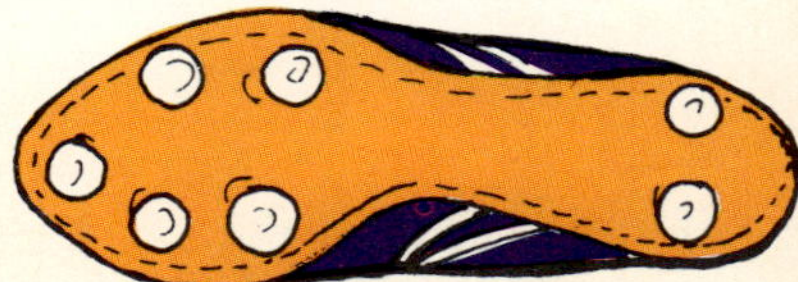
grass shoes with metal cleats

Jerseys are pulled on over the pads with help from teammates. They come in nylon with overstitched seams and also in *collegiate-cut* open fishnet, allowing for ventilation. *Breakaway* jerseys for running backs, flimsy things which will tear loose in a tackler's hands, are popular with punt-runbackers, some *scatbacks. Cost: $17-$22.*

Shoes are pulled on toward the end of the game-dressing procedure. Trainers call shoes the biggest pain in the ass in football equipment. Every athlete has his own idea of how low or high they should be cut—and wants to set fashion trends. Footwear became a publicity gimmick starting with **Joe Namath** of the New York Jets in 1966 and **Alvin Haymond** of the Baltimore Colts in the same period. Namath's *funky spats*, or white shoes, and Haymond's green jobs gained fame. Receivers, because they cut a lot, can go through 3 pairs in a season—*at costs ranging from $55 to $125 (custom-made) per pair.*

Armament

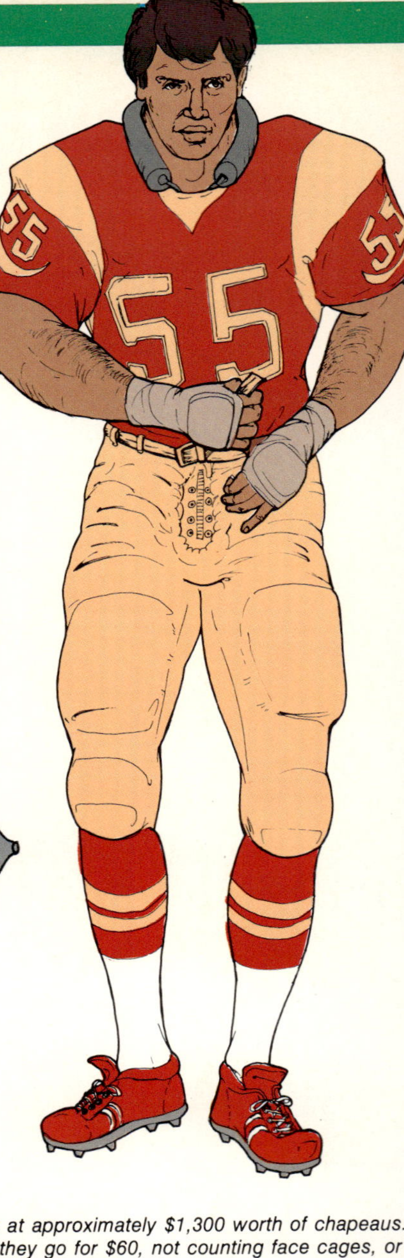

Helmets, face cages and mouthguards are the last to be donned—because they're hot and uncomfortable. Above the neck, players are protected by everything biophysical science can produce and still permit them to see what's going on. Helmets of the 1920s were skimpy, caplike arrangements of seasoned leather and straps, resembling an aviator's headpiece. By 1946 came the plastic shell with a new feature—the hard outside was separated from the skull by a suspension web. Science marched on to the plastic-molded model with improved suspension.

What you're looking at today is a 3-pound, highly sophisticated piece of polycarbonate, alloy, vinyl-foam, styrene and leather with an ingenious interior. Inside are pods which are filled with an antifreeze or other compound and arranged in a honeycomb. The liquid-filled cells absorb and distribute shocks to the head. The most widely used model, according to trainers, is the *Air Power® Helmet* produced by Bike® Athletic Co. of Knoxville, Tenn. It combines
1 dual protection of **air liners** or **pods**
2 and **foam stabilizers.** Eighty per cent of the Los Angeles Rams, for instance, wear the Air Power. An inner air liner is inflated
3 first with a **pump**—then, when the hat is on a player's head, a final inflation adjustment is made to an outer liner through an **air valve.**

3

After it's been used, it is simply rinsed out and wiped dry. "We figure to get 3 years of use out of a helmet," state the Rams. "Finally a hat gets so gouged and beat up that we have to retire it." (Players who are picked for the elite Pro Bowl are given their helmets as souvenirs.)

Whether it's an alcohol or antifreeze type, or an air-cushioned job, it's a lethal weapon. Manufacturers run notices: "WARNING. Do not use this helmet to butt, ram or spear an opposing player. This is in violation of football rules and can cause paralysis or death."

When 22 men line up for the kickoff, you're looking at approximately $1,300 worth of chapeaus. Ten years ago, a top-grade helmet cost $25. Now they go for $60, not counting face cages, or guards, at $10-$15 per set. If a giant lineman takes larger than an 8½ size hat, he needs to have one tailored—and that could run to $100 or more.

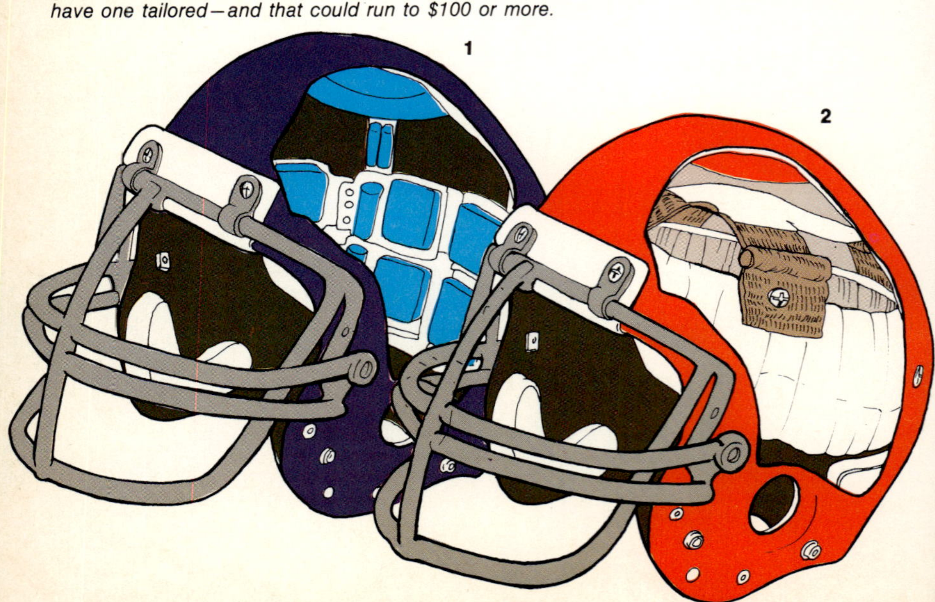

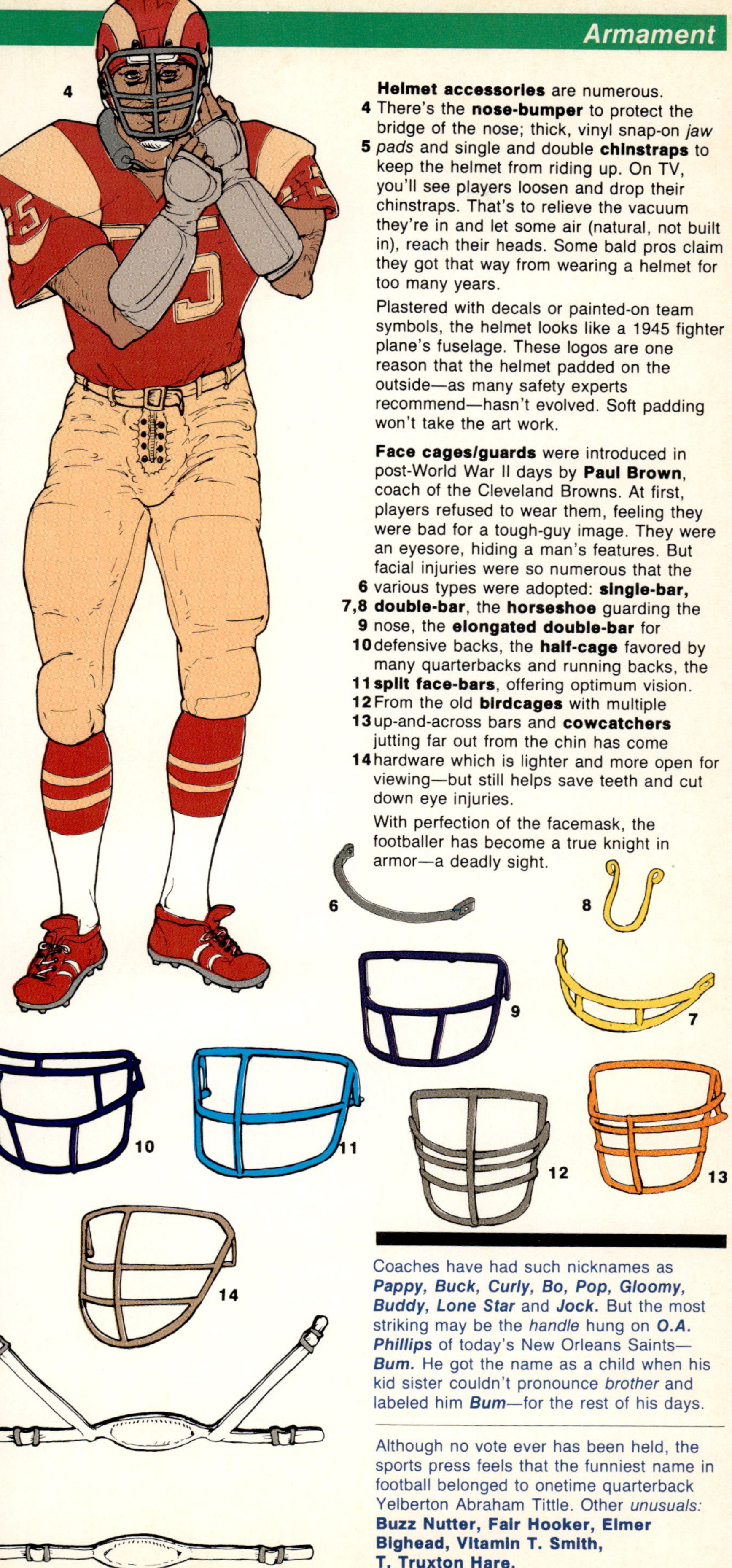

Helmet accessories are numerous.
4 There's the **nose-bumper** to protect the
bridge of the nose; thick, vinyl snap-on *jaw*
5 *pads* and single and double **chinstraps** to
keep the helmet from riding up. On TV, you'll see players loosen and drop their chinstraps. That's to relieve the vacuum they're in and let some air (natural, not built in), reach their heads. Some bald pros claim they got that way from wearing a helmet for too many years.

Plastered with decals or painted-on team symbols, the helmet looks like a 1945 fighter plane's fuselage. These logos are one reason that the helmet padded on the outside—as many safety experts recommend—hasn't evolved. Soft padding won't take the art work.

Face cages/guards were introduced in post-World War II days by **Paul Brown**, coach of the Cleveland Browns. At first, players refused to wear them, feeling they were bad for a tough-guy image. They were an eyesore, hiding a man's features. But facial injuries were so numerous that the
6 various types were adopted: **single-bar,**
7,8 **double-bar**, the **horseshoe** guarding the
9 nose, the **elongated double-bar** for
10 defensive backs, the **half-cage** favored by
many quarterbacks and running backs, the
11 **split face-bars**, offering optimum vision.
12 From the old **birdcages** with multiple
13 up-and-across bars and **cowcatchers**
jutting far out from the chin has come
14 hardware which is lighter and more open for
viewing—but still helps save teeth and cut down eye injuries.

With perfection of the facemask, the footballer has become a true knight in armor—a deadly sight.

Coaches have had such nicknames as ***Pappy, Buck, Curly, Bo, Pop, Gloomy, Buddy, Lone Star*** and ***Jock.*** But the most striking may be the *handle* hung on ***O.A. Phillips*** of today's New Orleans Saints—***Bum.*** He got the name as a child when his kid sister couldn't pronounce *brother* and labeled him ***Bum***—for the rest of his days.

Although no vote ever has been held, the sports press feels that the funniest name in football belonged to onetime quarterback Yelberton Abraham Tittle. Other *unusuals:* **Buzz Nutter, Fair Hooker, Elmer Bighead, Vitamin T. Smith, T. Truxton Hare.**

Armament

Mouthguards originally were patterned after those used by prize fighters—heavy and uncomfortable. Now a wax impression of a player's mouth is taken and a perfect fit obtained. Quarterbacks dislike mouthguards because they have to call signals and the rubber jobs interfere with their clear diction. But it beats having 3 or 4 front teeth knocked backward and into the roof of the mouth—as has happened.

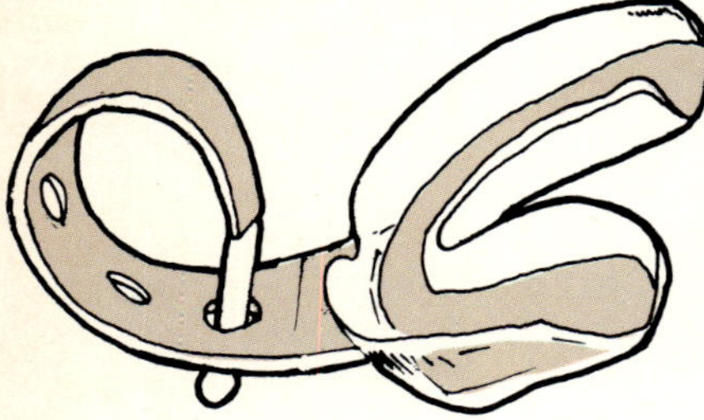

Trainer's aids: A Space Age look is given to the head trainer's side line pharmacy—called the *Crash Cart—by the EGS*® (Electrogalvanic Stimulator) and the *Neuromod Pulse Generator*®. These devices ease pain during combat. Then there's the *Sensory Isolation Tank*, where after games the players float in silent darkness in shallow water and get their ringing skulls and perception back together.

Other jazzy equipment: Coaches are experimenting with a baseball-type *radar gun* for ascertaining the velocity of a quarterback's pass. Speeds of 70 m.p.h. on *bullet* passes have been measured.

The Pittsburgh Steelers spent $1,400 for a bazooka-like *football ejector*, or kicking machine. The robot punter can kick a ball up to 400 feet with the spin of a right or left-footed kicker and adjust to wind currents.

In an Ottawa nightclub, according to press reports, the winner of a $1 lottery can throw a regulation brick through a TV screen showing TV commentator **Howard Cosell's** image. Sixteen TV sets are furnished and business is said to be brisk.

Illegal devices: Not so long ago, flattened beer cans were concealed under heavy forearm tape. They sent many a gridder to Cuckoo Land. Hidden metal was outlawed. Officials check before kickoffs to ensure that no metal or fiberglass is present and that 5/8ths-of-an-inch sponge padding covers any rigid materials.

***The total tab:** Counting such odds-and-ends as **belts, shoelaces, contact lenses, sideline capes** for foul weather, **practice pants** and **jerseys** and **team blazers** and **slacks** for travel, NFL owners spend $180,000 annually on equipment—about as much as the salaries of two first-string defensive linemen. Colleges get by with less. One major Pacific Coast university claims it spends no more than $50,000 to uniform a squad. Double that would be a more realistic figure.*

It shows up when school and NFL teams hit the road. They carry with them up to 2,500 pounds of baggage. Coming home, it weighs more. Don't forget the sweat the boys collect.

Five U.S. Presidents wore grid spangles.

Franklin Delano Roosevelt captained Harvard's freshman team in 1900.

Dwight D. Eisenhower was a starting Army halfback in 1912 until November 12, when a broken leg against the Carlisle Indians ended his career. In 1921, Ike coached the Army All-Stars.

Gerald Ford was Michigan U's *most valuable player* in 1934, playing the center position. (Green Bay offered the 210-pound Ford a pro tryout, which he declined.)

In 1937-38, **John F. Kennedy** was a pretty good pass-catching end for the Harvard freshman and junior varsity team.

Ronald Reagan played prep school ball. As an actor portraying Notre Dame's legendary **George Gipp** in a Warner Brothers movie, he sped 50 yards for a touchdown. *Gipp* then bounced the ball on the ground. That was in 1940 and Reagan thereby became the first recorded end-zone *spiker* of a football.

If you're reading **FOOTBALL**/ACCESS in the wintertime in the northern U.S., you can be sure that one of the following *antifreeze* devices or gear is in use on the sidelines:

Women's pantyhose worn next to the body for warmth. (Taupe is the players' favorite shade.) Also **thermal underwear**, tested for the Minnesota Vikings by a party of Mt. Everest climbers.

Chemical bag hand-warmers.

Battery-powered heaters taken onto the field during timeouts for instant warming of fingers numbed in zero weather.

Electric blankets installed under the turf to melt snow and reaching to the bench for foot-warming.

Electrically-heated benches or *hot seats*—first used by the New York Giants and Philadelphia Eagles.

Pouch pockets on uniform jerseys for between-play unfreezing of hands by QBs, runners and receivers.

Ladies' hair spray used as a water repellent for shoes on wet days.

St. Louis Cardinals-type ball-dryer, or an enclosed, heated drum that dries 7 balls at a time in rainy weather.

Baseball shirts worn under jerseys.

On the opposite type of day—boiling hot weather—**air-conditioning units**, as introduced by the University of Southern California at Alabama in 1977 at benchside.

All NFL teams are required to have **oxygen** and **instant X-ray equipment** at the stadium, either on the sideline or close by.

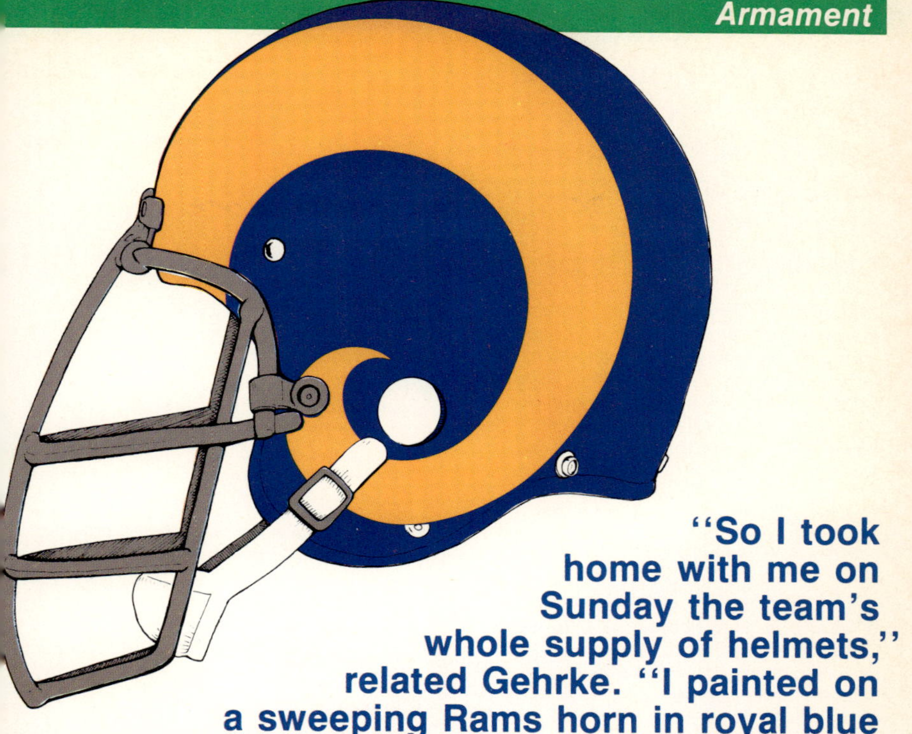

"So I took home with me on Sunday the team's whole supply of helmets," related Gehrke. "I painted on a sweeping Rams horn in royal blue and gold, our colors. I didn't know what would happen—whether the owners would be mad as hell at me or what."

The year was 1947. **Fred Gehrke**, a swivel-hipped Los Angeles Rams running back, and an art major, said he was tired of looking at plain, unadorned, uninspired combat *hats* worn by the pros.

Gehrke's idea was an instant hit with owners and fans. Other clubs rushed to the drawing board to design logos as nifty as that of the Rams. Both orthodox and wild ideas resulted.

In Baltimore, the Colts experimented with two small horseshoes at the rear of the helmet. When their customers approved, the Colts went to full-size shoes over both earholes. The Pittsburgh Steelers borrowed the three-star symbol of the steel industry. Minnesota's Viking horn and the Flying Wing of the Philadelphia Eagles followed.

Among off-the-wall emblems, which today come in the form of decals to be fixed to the hat, are a blue lion in Detroit, a helmet-wearing dolphin in Miami, a futuristic hawk in Seattle, a *fleur de lis* in New Orleans (resembling a peeled banana, some critics say) and a 1776 Minuteman in New England. Acts of nature include the San Diego Chargers' lightning streak and the Texas Star of Dallas.

Attempts to put bull's-eyes on headgear have been foiled. The NFL ruled that this would present too much of a target to the passer when worn by receivers.

Only one league team staunchly refuses to dress up its headdress: the Cleveland Browns. The Brownies alone wear plain, unadorned toppers.

Hold That Tiger!

War Eagle—Auburn U's huge eagle, trained to emit a scream when the team scores

Bevo—longhorn steer mascot of the Texas Longhorns

Albert the Alligator—a 12-foot-long swamp gator adopted by the Florida U Gators

Freddie Fang—Montana U's bobcat and TV star

Traveler III—a 16-hand Arabian horse who races around the Los Angeles Coliseum track when USC scores a touchdown. Maybe the most photographed mascot of them all

Ralphie—Colorado U's 1,500-pound American bison, the largest mascot in captivity

Mike—Louisiana State's snarling Bengal tiger

Ab and Daisy—Baylor's twin bear cubs who live in a luxurious $2500 campus domicile

Bill XXVII—latest in a series of Navy's long line of *good luck* goats, dating to 1890

Ragnar—300 pounds of untamed boar which mascots for the Arkansas U football squad and chases people up trees

Black athletes now comprise 55 per cent of NFL rosters. The first black quarterback in pro annals was the aptly-named **Willie Thrower** of the Chicago Bears in 1953. The first black to become an NFL coach was **Emlen Tunnell**, a defensive marvel with the New York Giants and Green Bay Packers from 1948-61. Tunnell joined the Giants' tutoring staff in 1965.

Weights & Measures

Along with increase of the Gross National Product, footballers continue to expand in height, weight and girth. Record-keepers agree that the most mammoth gladiator yet to come along was *Bob Pointer*, a 487-pound tackle who played in Santa Barbara and Arizona in the 1960

Pointer didn't make it to the pro league because of slowness. But 300-pounders are much in demand. Such behemoths aren't uncommon in an age when some NFL defensive lines average 275 pounds per man. The Kansas City Chiefs, in one Super Bowl match, fielded the following 3 middle linemen:

Defensive tackle **Buck Buchanan**, 6′7″, 300 lbs.
Offensive tackle **Jim Tyrer**, 6′6″, 295 lbs.
Defensive tackle **Ernie Ladd**, 6′9″, 305 lbs.

No set of tackles has ever come bigger than that and probably won't in the future. Most coaches of today prefer their front-line shock troops to be built along the modified design of the huge but agile, fast-moving **John Hannah** of the New England Patriots or **Mark Gastineau** of the New York Jets. Both Hannah and Gastineau can cover 40 yards in under 5 seconds and are superstars of the 1980s.

Hannah (offensive guard)—6′3″, 275 pounds. His chest measures 52″; his thighs, 33″; his neck, 22″. "He splits helmets", say New England coaches of Hannah, who dieted down from 306 pounds and 4 times has been named *Most Valuable Lineman* by vote of NFL players.

Gastineau (defensive end)—6′5″, 290 pounds. His shoe size is 16 and his biceps outmeasure those of most wrestlers. In one afternoon he sacked Houston quarterback **Ken Stabler** 4 times. Has been known to tear an opponent's facemask loose from its screws with his great paws.

During the 1940s-1960s, men of tremendous size appeared throughout the NFL. Example: **Sherman Plunkett**, the 335-pound *world's largest tackle*, who protected Quarterback **Joe Namath** for the N.Y. Jets. But pro thinking changed. The ideal lineman of the '80s is more streamlined, combining quick reaction, recovery speed and strength. Typical of the top names, along with Hannah and Gastineau, are:

Mike Webster, Pittsburgh center—called *the strongest man in football*, he's 6′2″, 250 pounds. Can bench-press 400 pounds. The ideal size for a ball-snapper, Webster almost never is injured.

Randy White, Dallas defensive tackle—6′4″, 255 pounds, White, year in and out, is the best player on the Cowboy squad. A ferocious pass-rusher, teammates call him *Manster*, for half-man, half-monster.

Jack Youngblood, Los Angeles Rams defensive end—6′4″, 250 pounds. So tough that he played in 2 playoff games with a broken leg bone in a cast. "I eat quarterbacks", says Youngblood.

Jack Lambert, Pittsburgh linebacker—Godzilla as a middle linebacker. At 6′4″, 225 pounds, Lambert is known for his tooth-rattling tackles.

Leon Gray, Houston offensive tackle—6′3″, 270 pounds. Pries open holes which have made Earl Campbell one of the NFL's premier ground-gainers. Considered one of 3 best in the NFL at position.

Although none of the above 5 prototype linemen weighs more than 270, this doesn't mean that the era of the Goodyear blimp in human form has sailed out of football. Some linemen are so vast that they require a double seat on the team airplane and eat 4 kingsize steaks at a sitting:

Milt Hardaway, Detroit tackle—6′9″, 340 lbs.
Jerry Wilkinson, 49ers defensive end—6′9″, 275 lbs.
Dale Markham, Giants defensive end—6′8″, 280 lbs.
Billy Shields San Diego tackle—6′8″, 275 lbs.
Phil Murphy, Rams tackle—6′6″, 305 lbs.
Wilbur Young, Redskins defensive end—6′6″, 295 lbs.

Size by position

Offensive guards are the smallest of the linemen because they need sprinter speed to pull out and run interference for backs on sweep plays, and the quickness to handle defensive tackles. Average: 6′2″, 240-255 pounds.

Defensive tackles are man mountains because they're double-teamed by a guard-center or center-tackle tandems. Still, they must be able to rush the passer in 3 to 5 seconds. Average: 6′3″- 6′4″, 260-270 pound

Defensive ends usually are taller, lighter and faster off the mark than DT's; they must not try to overpower defensive tackles, but must maneuver around them to reach the passer from the outside. Average: 6′5″- 6′6″, 250 pounds.

Offensive tackles are superdreadnoughts, with the job of delaying pass-rushers and firing out to wedge open holes for runners. Average: 6′6″, 265-275 pounds.

Linebackers must hit with the force of a tackle when charging up to plug holes in the line. They must also have speed to range left and right against sweeps, plus sprinter celerity to run blitzes on the quarterback. No real monsters wanted here. Average: 6′3″, 225-235 pounds.

Probably the biggest man in college action today is defensive tackle **Jim Polk** of Grambling University—**6′9″** and **325** pounds. Polk wears size **16** shoes and an **8½**-size helmet. He rivals **335**-pound **Angelo Fields**, an offensive tackle with the Houston Oilers of the NFL. "It's a good cab ride or a 2-day walk to get around him," they say of Fields.

The pro QB is growing bigger.

The 6-foot-tall passer is becoming a rarity. In the past, **Johnny Unitas, Bart Starr** and **Fran Tarkenton** were *little* QBs who had great success. But then came **Roger Staubach** (6′3″, 210 lbs.) and **Terry Bradshaw** (6′3″, 215 lbs.) in the early 1970s to set a trend of tall men who could see over the charging defense and had the bone structure to withstand monstrous tacklers. Among today's largest quarterbacks are:

Don Strock, *Miami*-6′5″, 220 lbs.
Lynn Dickey, *Green Bay*-6′4″, 220 lbs.
Steve Bartkowski, *Atlanta*-6′4″, 215 lbs.
Craig Morton, *Denver*-6′4″, 215 lbs.
Dan Fouts, *San Diego*-6′3½″, 210 lbs.
Ken Anderson, *Cincinnati*-6′3″, 215 lbs.
Mike Livingston, *Kansas City*-6′4″, 210 lbs.
Archie Manning, *New Orleans*-6′3″, 205 lbs.

There were mighty men in the past, but not as many monsters were around as today.

On the average, the oldtimers lacked the bulk of the *whales* of the 1980s. A list of some of the biggest men ever to take the field, by era:

The tallest: 7′0″

The shortest: 5′4″

1920s:
Cal Hubbard (T), 6′5″, 255 lbs.
N.Y. Giants and other teams

1930s:
Joe Stydahar (T), 6′4″, 260 lbs.
Chicago Bears

1940s:
Al Blozis (T), 6′7″, 260 lbs.
N.Y. Giants

1950s:
Bob St. Clair (T), 6′9″, 265 lbs.
San Francisco 49ers

1960s:
Les Bingaman (G-T), 6′3″, 310 lbs.
Detroit Lions
Doug Atkins (DE), 6′8″, 270 lbs.
Cleveland Browns, Chicago Bears, New Orleans Saints

1970s:
Lamar Lundy (DE), 6′7″, 260 lbs.
L.A. Rams
Carl Eller (DE), 6′6″, 265 lbs.
Minnesota Vikings
Ernie Ladd (T), 6′9″, 270 lbs.
Kansas City Chiefs
Buck Buchanan (T), 6′7″, 290 lbs.
Kansas City Chiefs
Jim Tyrer (T), 6′6″, 295 lbs.
Kansas City Chiefs
Bob Brown (T), 6′5″, 300 lbs.
Green Bay Packers, Oakland Raiders
Ben Davidson (DE), 6′7″, 280 lbs.
Oakland Raiders

1980s:
L.C. Greenwood (DE), 6′7″, 270 lbs.
Pittsburgh Steelers
Leroy Jones (DE), 6′8″, 265 lbs.
San Diego Chargers
Ed *Too Tall* Jones (DE), 6′9″, 270 lbs.
Dallas Cowboys
John Matuszak (DE), 6′8″, 275 lbs.
Oakland Raiders
Dick Sligh (T), 7′0″, 300 lbs.
Cincinnati Bengals

Small Tony Dorsett of the Dallas Cowboys holds the NFL record for most consecutive seasons of gaining 1,000 or more yards (5, from 1977 through 1981). Fans marvel that a man of only 5′11″ and 190 pounds can survive to reach All-Pro rank.

Anyone who considers Dorsett undersized hasn't studied the subject. Number 33 for the Cowboys is a big boy compared to some of the tiny types who've overcome long odds to become heroes.

Among the most astonishing peewees:

Eddie LeBaron—at 5′7″ and 160 pounds, he was the ace quarterback for 10 years for the Washington Redskins and Dallas Cowboys. LeBaron quarterbacked a 1956 winning Pro Bowl squad, which led 6′9″, 300-pound *Big Daddy* Lipscomb to snarl, You little S.O.B.—I'll get you one of these years!"

Buddy Young—an Olympic-class sprinter who at 5′5″, 160, sped and swiveled for many touchdowns with the Dallas Texans and Baltimore Colts.

Charley Tolar—"Like trying to catch a bowling ball," they said of the hydrant-shaped, 5′6″, 190-pound Tolar of the Houston Oilers in the 1960s.

Noland *Supergnat* Smith—an invisible 5′5½″, Supergnat holds several NFL records, set in the 1960s. One of them is for the longest runback of a kickoff—106 yards. Starred with the Kansas City Chiefs.

Randy Vataha—the New England Patriots' miniature wide receiver was so tiny he once played *Bashful* of the Seven Dwarfs at Disneyland. Stadium guards, unable to believe he was a player, refused admission to Vataha. In his first pro season, Randy caught 51 passes and scored 9 touchdowns.

As of 1982, the smallest performer in pro football (the shortest ever) is the incredible runback specialist of the Atlanta Falcons—**Reggie *The Elf* Smith.** Reggie's all of 5 feet, 4 inches tall.

Injuries-The Ultimate Factor

"More than talent, teaching, scouting, recruiting or breaks of the game, *injuries are the most important factor in deciding championships.*"

So said Coach Don Shula of the Miami Dolphins. So many players are crippled each season that the situation has been termed an epidemic. Team trainers—once important—now are only aides to orthopedic surgeons and post-operation therapists. Four or 5 knee operations are common among players. Some pros have gone under the knife as many as 8 times.

Since 1974, the NFL has legislated rules aimed to cut down violence and maiming of its men. Efforts have been successful to a degree. But modern gridders are bigger by 20-25 pounds than those of 30 years ago. Linemen weighing 270 can run 40 yards in 4.9 seconds—almost as fast as yesterday's heavier running backs.

Tests by physicists show that when 2 giants collide at headlong speed, the kinetic energy they release could move 33 tons one inch.

Stanford Research Institute surveys indicate that until changes are made in the hard-shell helmet and other equipment and *maniac* players are brought under tighter control, injuries will not substantially decrease. This means your favorite team is in the hands of fate...luck...call it what you will.

Although the overwhelming majority of injuries sustained by football players are simple sprains and minor contusions, the most common **major** football injury involves the **medial collateral ligaments** which connect the upper leg bone to the lower leg bone at the knee. Usually caused by a severe blow to the outside of the knee that either tears the ligament away from the bone or creates a tear in the ligament itself, this injury frequently requires surgery.

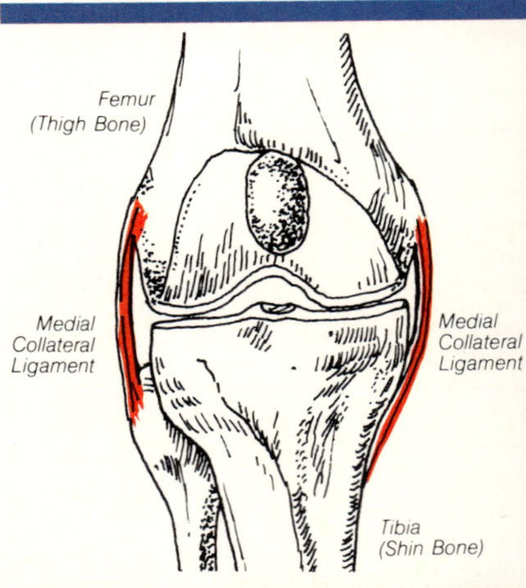

Facts from recent NFL seasons

The Detroit Lions set a record when 21 players underwent knee surgery in a single season.

Six Oakland Raiders were hospitalized after one game.

The Los Angeles Rams were decimated in 1981, losing such starters as **Doug France, Larry Brooks, Pat Haden, Jackie Slater** and **Irv Pankey** to serious injuries.

Big names have been forced into early retirement: Miami quarterback **Bob Griese**; Pittsburgh tackle ***Mean Joe* Greene**; Miami safetyman **Tim Foley; Gayle Sayers**, Chicago's triplethreat runner, among many.

Craig Morton, Denver Cowboys' veteran passer, following 4 knee operations, played in '81 with tendons taken from his foot and transplanted in his shoulder so that he could throw again.

San Francisco 49ers lost their No.1 runner, **Paul Hofer**, permanently; Houston's power runner, **Earl Campbell**, was sidelined for a time; all-pro **Bill Bergey** of Philadelphia was injured and is now retired.

Jim Otto of Oakland (10 broken noses, broken jaw, 3 left-knee operations and 6 right-knee operations) had to retire. Otto made the Hall of Fame.

The casualty rate: a New York Jets study disclosed that linemen in *The Pit* (line center) are injured once every 368 plays. Kamikazes are hurt once every 103 plays. Special teamers **Stone Johnson** of Kansas City (1963) and **Chuck Hughes** of Detroit (1971) died on the field.

Special teams. For short periods, members of the *Suicide, Banzai* or *Kamikaze* units have the most dangerous duty of all. To operate here, you must like it bloody. Special teams are composed of rookies, expendable second-stringers and other backup types. They race down under kickoffs to meet the defense with boxcar impact. When the kickoff's return pattern veers toward the sidelines, the field becomes a patchwork of bodies meeting at odd and frequently blind angles. Invisible hits are featured. Also foul play. In another special-teams area—punt returns—the action is less spread, but almost as violent.

Famous special units: the *Doomsday Squad* (Baltimore Colts), *Guillory's Gorillas* (L.A. Rams), the *Wild Bunch* (Washington Redskins), *Haymond's Headhunters* (L.A. Rams).

Kamikaze squads developed as a tactical refinement in the 1950s. They multiplied until they now include up to 8 groups: a point-after-touchdown rushing team, onside-kick defense team, field goal kicking and defending teams, punting and punt-comeback teams, kickoff coverage and return teams.

In 1981, ***Sovietskii Sport*** published this about American football: "It is impossible not to shudder at the players' cruelty...any of them can commit an act of cruelty, but only a handful can do it before 60,000 people without being detected."

Most violent tactics

Blind-side hit: Used on QBs in the act of completing a throw and on a tailback receiving an option-play pass from the QB and unable to see onrushing tackler.

Chop-blocking: Vicious blocking down to the knees when a man is held by a teammate and is in a rigid or off-balance position.

Clubbing or *bouncer's wallop:* Illegal jawbreaker delivered via a smash of arm and fists to neck. Use of it against receiver Lynn Swann of Pittsburgh led Coach Chuck Noll to charge that a "criminal element" was loose in the sport.

Crackback block: Illegal since 1976 in college play and since 1978 in NFL play, this is a clip delivered at or near the scrimmage line by an end slanting back in from the outside.

Ear-holing: Aiming the crown of the head at a player's ear with devastating result.

Head-butting: Illegal since 1979, but still common. Grabbing jersey, pulling forward and following with a sharp blow to head.

Leg-whipping: Offensive lineman, having failed on a block, reaches back with his legs and flails them across a man's shins.

Rake-blocking: Ramming opponent's chest, then whipping the facemask up to the chin.

Spearing: Outlawed by colleges in 1970. This is the deliberate use of the helmet to punish a man, whether stopped or not. Pros now have a rule on this. **Example:** in a notorious 1978 incident, **Jack *Black Death* Tatum** (Oakland safetyman) *stuck it to* **Darryl Stingley** (New England receiver). Stingley was left permanently paralyzed.

Meanies, brutes, the toughest guys

The *villain championship* is much in dispute. Aggression is the most marketable asset of any player and some individuals carry hard hitting to the point that they become *intimidators by fear*. These streetfighters say they are only doing a violent job the best way they know how. But dirty tactics cost many yards in officials' penalties and breed more dirty play in the form of retaliation. It's a thin line between normal mayhem and the type of tactics which former Chicago Bears' center **Jon Morris** predicted "will kill the game in the long run".

Anyone with a cursory knowledge of the game and who sits in the stands or watches on TV can detect hitting after the whistle, kicking a downed man, illegal headhunting tackles, kneeing, deliberate clips and so on. "A thousand times I heard guys say they'd end my career any way they could", stated a retired **Johnny Unitas**. So did **Walter Payton**, one of the greatest runners. Unitas managed to survive for 17 years. Payton's career was ended by injuries soon after it flowered.

Complicating the problem, not all classic *meanies* use unsportsmanlike methods, but rather hurt people out of sheer, natural ferocity. If a Hall of Fame of intimidators was formed, it would include these gridiron wild men:

Hardy *The Hatchet* Brown (San Francisco, 1950s) In one season, linebacker Brown caused 21 men to be carried off the field. Not big at 190 pounds, he KO'd them with a unique uppercut of his shoulderpads.

Dick Butkus (Chicago Bears, 1960s-70s) Made the Hall of Fame over a trail of wrecked bodies. Called *The Animal*, linebacker Butkus once was charged with biting a referee.

Les Richter (Los Angeles Rams, 1950s-60s) "So mean he frightened himself", they said of this big linebacker; the Rams traded 11 players to obtain Richter in a celebrated deal.

Joe Schmidt (Detroit Lions, 1950s-60s) He was as violent as Butkus and even more creative. He tore the pants clear off Rams' quarterback Roman Gabriel with his hands and teeth.

At present and in the recent past, the villains who made the most lurid headlines have been:

Mike Curtis, (Baltimore Colts) Linebacker who was such a wild man that he was thrown out of games—and even out of practice sessions for fighting with his own teammates.

Joe *Mean* Joe Greene, (Pittsburgh Steelers) The same *nice guy* who gave the little kid his jersey in a prizewinning Coca-Cola commercial on TV, he was ejected from games for stomping on officials, groin-kicking and clubbing. Mean Joe's name goes down in history.

Conrad Dobler, (St. Louis Cardinals) Guard: *Mr. Violence* from coast to coast. During a pre-game coin toss, Dobler punched one of the enemy in the head. The NFL's *most unpopular* in 1981 by a wide margin.

Johnny Sample, (Baltimore Colts, Washington Redskins, N.Y. Jets) Sample titled his autobiography *The Confessions of a Dirty Ballplayer*. He was *The Baddest of Them All*, a defensive back who intercepted passes and then threw the ball into the faces of opposing coaches.

Playing Field

Under the game's original *Princeton Rules,* the field was 120 yards long.

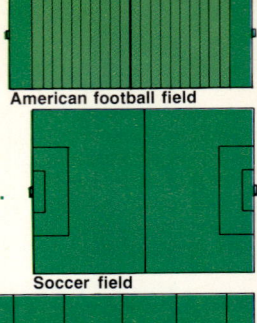

Light green = 1 acre

American football field

Soccer field

It still is, but the action is concentrated in the center 100 yards.
1 The other 20 yards is end zone real estate—10 yards of **EZ** behind each goal line. End zones are **scoring** territory—where the ball must be advanced by rush, pass or other means in order to put points on the board. The field's width is **53.333 yards**, or **160 feet.** Because of the increased size and speed of players and because the zone passing defense has cut down long TD passes, a 65-yard-wide field, as in Canadian football, has been suggested.

2 **Side lines:** The entire field of play is bordered by a solid white line, 6 feet wide; only the area within the sidelines and endlines is **inbounds.** That is, if a player steps on **any part** of the white line, he's out-of-bounds. Doesn't seem fair, but that's it.

in out

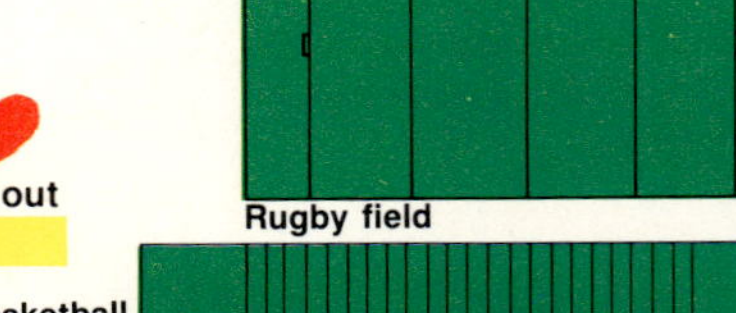

Rugby field

Basketball

Tennis

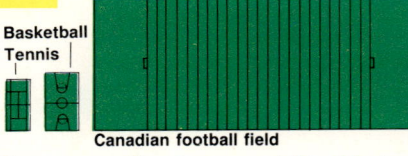

Canadian football field

3 **Inbounds lines** or ***hashmarks:*** In 1972, the NFL moved the hashmarks (small vertical lines) closer to the middle of the field to 23 yards, 1 foot and 9 inches from each sideline—an increase of 10 feet, 9 inches on either side. The ball is put in play on a hashmark if the preceding play ended wide of the hashmark. This was done as a boost to the running game, offering added room for wide plays. And the running game prospered. Suddenly, the number of backs gaining 1,000 yards per season shot up.

This change leaves 18 feet, 6 inches between the hashmarks in the middle of the field, which happens to be the exact width of the goalposts in pro football. In college ball, the hashmarks are 53 feet, 4 inches from each sideline, compared to 70 feet, 9 inches for the pros.

Yardage chain: The chain is 10 yards long when fully extended, joined by 2 rods at least 5 feet high. It's used to measure whether 10 yards, or less, have been gained on a down. Built in is a down-indicator on a rod 4 feet high, holding 4 cards numbered 1, 2, 3 and 4 (downs progressively). The indicator marks the most forward point of the ball at the start of each down. A 3-to-4 man team runs the chain. *A chain-indicator set costs $400.*

4 **Yard lines:** These are plastic-painted or chalked at 5-yard intervals parallel to the goal lines, with intervening yards shown by 1-yard markers. A yard line has nothing to do with offense, but is spoken of in terms of the defending team. **Example:** If Ohio State is in possession at its own 35-yard line, it is 35 yards upfield from the goal it is defending. When teams change ends at the start of a new quarter, identity of the yard lines changes with them.

5 **PAT markers:** These white markers on point-after-touchdown tries are placed on the 3-yard line by the colleges, the 2-yard line by the NFL.

Flags: In 1965, the color of NFL officials' penalty flags was changed from white to bright gold—easier to see against green turf and on color TV. Field flags are supplied by stadium management. Eight are required—1 at each side line of the goal line and one at each corner extremity of the end zone.

6 **Team areas:** Benches are set 5 to 6 feet from the sidelines and, by rule, team areas should contain only authorized personnel. But everyone and his Aunt Minnie seems to congregate here. The bench is the worst seat in the house, by the way (too low down), which is why coaches rely on press-box-stationed assistants to analyze what's going on and to recommend plays by phone. Bench area is defined as between the 35-yard lines.

Dog patrol: Colleges, which get a lot of stray canines on the field, employ students armed with everything from doggie bones to nets.

Are phone lines ever tapped by opponents? The Los Angeles Rams once accused the Chicago Bears of listening in. And phones have gone dead at critical moments.

Goalposts: Padded with kapok or foam rubber, *posts*, or *standards*, have changed in design and location. For years they formed a letter **H.** Now they're a broad-based **U**, offset and called *slingshot.* In 1967, the NFL (for safety) set the upright legs behind the end line of the end zone, but with the crossbar portion extended exactly to the end line. Fans destroyed so many in postgame celebrations that now the posts are sunk in cement (but sometimes still crash down for souvenirs). The pro rule is that vertical posts must extend 30 ft. above the crossbar, for better judging by officials on field goals and conversion kicks. And they must be bright gold in color.

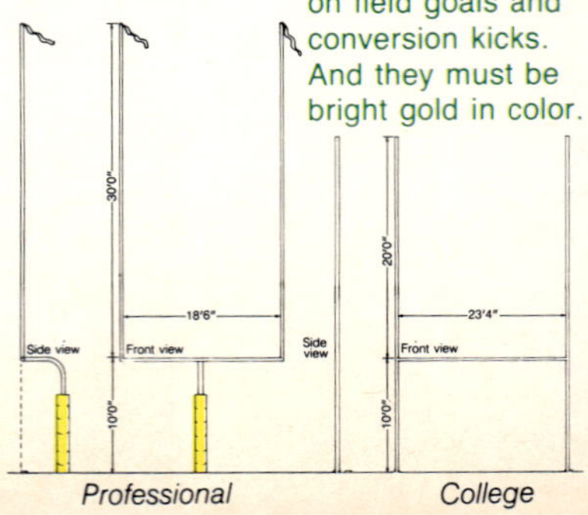

Playing Field

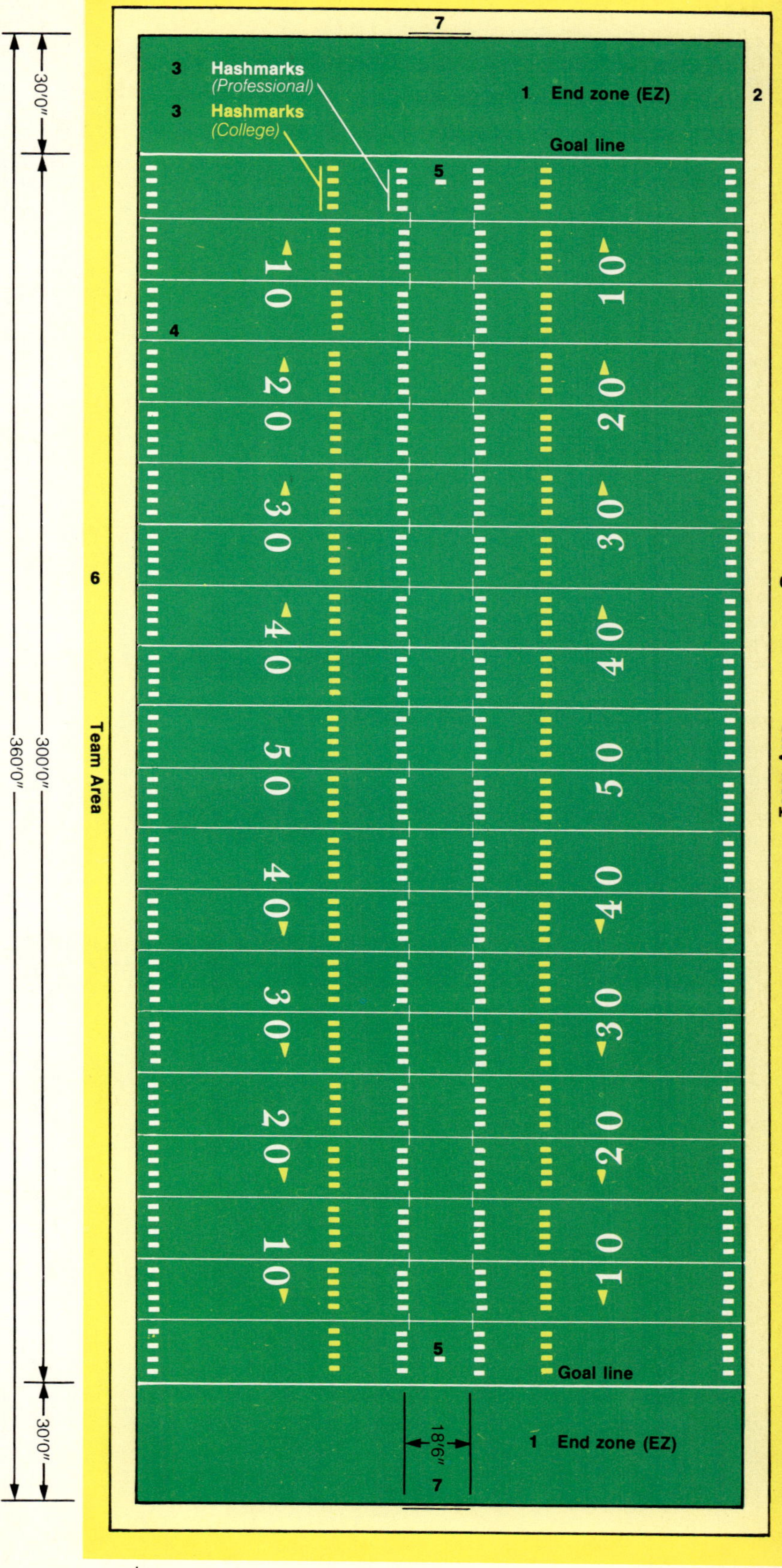

The Time Factor

Time in relation to football is a unique thing. It has nothing to do with Greenwich Mean, 60 minutes to an hour or any other normal measurement. Gridiron time is indefinite, expandable and uncertain—until the final gun.

Games are 60 minutes in length, rulewise. They are divided into 4 15-minute quarters. Yet the typical contest runs more than 150 minutes, or just over 2½ hours. This is due to:

1. A wide assortment of **time-outs** in which the clock is stopped.
2. A 15-minute or longer **halftime intermission** and 2-minute **intervals between the quarters.**
3. A 25- to 30-second period for the attacking team to put the ball into play on each of **60 to 75 plays** per game.
4. Television's encroachment. Sixteen or more **commercial messages** per game of 30 to 60 seconds duration usually come during regular, game-connected time-outs, but sometimes require added *TV time-outs*. In the latter case, a CBS, NBC or ABC network agent standing on the side line signals the referee that a *special* pause is needed for a sales pitch. One signal often used is the placing of the agent's hand over his heart, to which the referee responds by halting the action long enough for Madison Avenue to do its thing. Selling the product has priority where TV sport is concerned. In one Super Bowl game a kickoff was actually replayed because TV wasn't ready and missed filming it.
5. Delaying tactics in the final stages of a game. This is called the **2-minute drill**. In this phase, the scheduled 2-minute finale frequently drags out to a 15- to 20-minute finale while coaches try in various ways to beat the clock.
   Example: The Oakland Raiders and New York Jets once struggled at such length—for 3 hours—that NBC cut off the telecast with 90 seconds left. That final 90 seconds lasted 12 more minutes. (See *2-Minute Drill* later in this section.)
6. **Sudden-death overtime** in case of a tie finish. In NFL games, this is composed of a 3-minute rest period after regulation time has run out. Then come 15-minute periods of play until one team scores and thus wins the game. There are 2-minute intervals between these subsequent periods.

A recent trend in pro and collegiate ball is for contests to drag out for 3 hours. A multiplicity of time-out situations is the main factor here. These are the main instances when the clock stops ticking:

- After an **incomplete pass.**
- After a **score**—either touchdown, field goal, extra point conversion or safety.
- During a **team time-out.** Each team is allowed 3 time-outs of **2 minutes duration** per half, or a total of 12 for both sides per game. This amounts to a total of 24 minutes.
- During a **rules infraction** and the following measurement and applied penalty.
- **After a kickoff.** About 3 minutes *normal time* is allowed for the kick-receiving special team to leave the field in favor of the offensive team.
- When a player in possession of the ball **steps out-of-bounds**, either voluntarily or from being pushed out.
- When a ball is **thrown out-of-bounds.**
- During an unusual situation and **at the referee's discretion**, such as fans on the field, malfunction of the official clock or crowd booing so intense that the quarterback's signal calls can't be heard by his mates. *Free*, extra time-outs may be allowed in the uproar, sometimes 2, 3 or even 4 of them.

What with all these interruptions in the action, many fans overlook the fact that the ball is in actual *live* play for only **12-15** minutes out of the prescribed 60 minutes. This is a difficult fact to believe. It takes less time to run a play than you'd think.

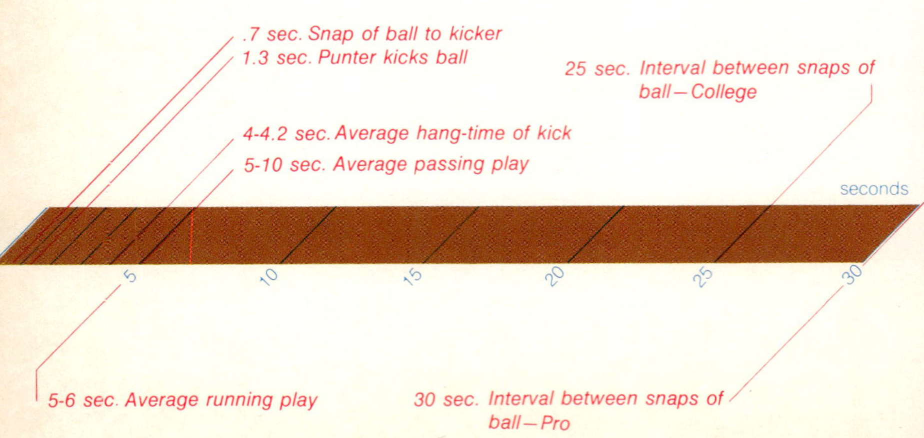

The Time Factor

For example:

- An **average passing down** takes but **5-10** seconds.
- An **average running play** takes **5-7** seconds. Although the clock keeps running during a rushing play, the time interval between one center snap to the next snap uses up just **30-45** seconds.

Speeding things up, the NFL allows **30** seconds to get the **ball into play** (or you're penalized **5** yards for delay of game). Colleges allow **25** seconds (thereby giving their customers about **10** per cent more plays per season than the NFL).

A little-known timing detail: As earlier mentioned, time-outs are for 2 minutes, except in such cases as an injury, when added time is given for medical inspection and removal of the injured man. When there is a regular time-out, the 30 second period allotted to execute the next play begins 1½ minutes into the time-out, not after the 2 minutes have elapsed.

Side line conferences: *Summit meetings* between quarterbacks, coaches and the offensive coordinator on a press box phone usually occur during injury, TV or other time-outs not charged to a team. When run past 2 minutes and turned into a debate, the referee moves in and orders the QB back to work. "We hate to see 5 or 6 coaches all putting in their nickel's worth to the QB instead of doing it the Dallas Cowboy way with one man (head coach Tom Landry) doing the talking," say officials.

2-minute drill or **final 2 minutes of each half:** On any kickoff in this late-stage time frame, the clock doesn't start until the ball has been touched by a player of either team (in all other cases, the clock starts with the actual kick). Also, on time-outs, the 3-time-outs-per-half rule is liberalized. A fourth time-out without penalty is allowed for an injury.

The 2-minute drill closing out each half consists of a hurry-up offense to get in as many plays as possible. It's bombs-away time. Snappy *out* (side line) passes are featured. These enable a receiver to jump out-of-bounds after a catch, killing the clock.

Huddles often are dispensed with, and the QB yelps his plays as fast as his linemen can get into position. QBs deliberately throw out-of-bounds as a clock-stopper when no receiver is open. This can be illegal, called *intentional grounding*, and earn a penalty, but only the most blatant grounding cases are penalized by officials.

QB's can stretch a 2-minute drill into 10 times that many minutes with mostly passing (stops clock) and side line *outs*. **Roger Staubach** (Dallas) came from behind 14 times in his career to win games in the final 2 minutes. Special stunts are saved for 2-minute football, when a trailing club desperately needs a field goal or touchdown.

In this frantic period, the *prevent defense* is thrown up against a shower of passes. Here, only 3 linemen may rush in while 5 to 7 men fade back to shut off a touchdown throw. Five men back is called a *nickel* alignment, 6 is a *dime* and 7 is a *red cent*. Or an *opposite prevent* may be employed. Eight men will charge in hope of sacking the QB or a running back, leaving the rear wide open to the pass. That's called the *Grits Blitz* by Atlanta's Falcons, *Death's Door* in Chicago and the *Maniac Charge* elsewhere.

Mechanics of timing. Even the Olympic Games don't have a better system for tallying the minutes and seconds. In football, the *Head Timer* and *Assistant Timer* sit either in the press box or on side line risers with a foot-long timing device which resembles a long switchboard panel. They push buttons, flick switches and turn dials to record the elapsed time of each down and the aggregate running time; in case of an equipment malfunction, the *Line Judge* carries a stopwatch as backup.

The 30-second clock is supervised by the *Field Judge*. Working under him and seated on the side line are 2 men using a hand-timing mechanism. This device is wired to each of the large (visible-to-the-crowd), 30-second clocks located at either side of the end zone. The 30-second clock can't be located on the scoreboard because it needs to be seen quickly and so is at eye-level to the quarterbacks. The EZ display clocks are digital and can be read with a glance.

Using his stopwatch, the *Field Judge* also keeps track of all time-outs and time between periods.

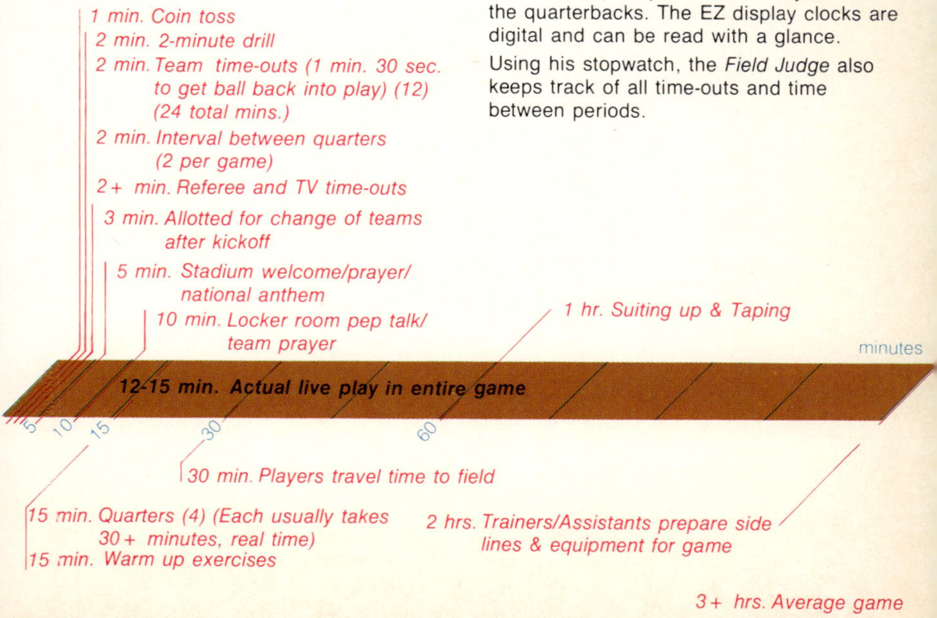

1 min. Coin toss
2 min. 2-minute drill
2 min. Team time-outs (1 min. 30 sec. to get ball back into play) (12) (24 total mins.)
2 min. Interval between quarters (2 per game)
2+ min. Referee and TV time-outs
3 min. Allotted for change of teams after kickoff
5 min. Stadium welcome/prayer/ national anthem
10 min. Locker room pep talk/ team prayer
1 hr. Suiting up & Taping
minutes
12-15 min. Actual live play in entire game
5 10 15 30 60
30 min. Players travel time to field
15 min. Quarters (4) (Each usually takes 30+ minutes, real time)
15 min. Warm up exercises
2 hrs. Trainers/Assistants prepare side lines & equipment for game
3+ hrs. Average game

Terms

Gridiron jargon began in the 1870s with such expressions as *Deadman's Play* (hidden ball), *limp leg* (technique for shaking off tacklers), and *Flying Wedge* (a V-shaped offensive formation).

It developed for two chief reasons:
1. Jargon was a verbal shorthand, allowing something to be described quickly.
2. It's an American trait to use colorful lingo.

Audible: change of play by the QB at the scrimmage line when he finds the original play won't work. Also called *automatic*.

Ax: defensive player's block on a wide receiver to disturb his maneuvering pattern.

Belly Series: QB's handoff to a running back in which he holds the ball in the runner's belly for a count before releasing the ball or switching it to another back.

Ben: block by a running back on a defensive end.

Blitz: defensive rush by linebackers and/or defensive backs aimed at smearing a developing play. A gamble, the blitz also is called a *red dog*.

Bootleg: QB fakes handoff to another back, hides ball on hip and carries ball himself.

Bump-and-Run: tactic by cornerback to slow pass receiver as he leaves scrimmage line.

Buttonhook: pass pattern where receiver runs straight, then hooks back to catch ball.

Chip shot: short field goal, under 20 yards.

Claws: good hands on a receiver.

C.O.D.: change of direction by a running back.

Coffin Corner: 3-5-yard area where the side line meets the goal line and where punters try to kick the ball out, avoiding a touchback.

Containing Defense: defensive strategy that will allow small gains in order to prevent a long gain.

Crap-roll Spike: after scoring, to bend on a knee and, pretending the ball is a pair of dice, roll it along the grass. Invented by Harold Carmichael of the Philadelphia Eagles.

Deke: runner's fake. Also *juke*.

Double Wing: formation which places 2 set backs at opposite ends of the field, spread out wide.

Down and Out: receiver pattern that extends straight down the field and outward to the side line at a 90-degree angle.

Draw Play: running play which starts out like a pass, but turns into a delayed running play as the quarterback hands off to a back. Used in obvious passing situations to catch defense off guard and draw it in.

End Around: play where an end circles back through the backfield, while the team's motion tends to go the opposite way. The end receives the ball on this reverse play.

Fair Catch: catch of a punt, signaled by a raised arm, in which the receiver may not run the ball back, but neither may he be tackled.

Far Side: television term meaning side farther from the camera.

Fire-out: offensive lineman's quick charge at snap of the ball.

Flat Pass: short pass thrown out to a receiver off to the side a few yards past the line of scrimmage.

Floating Pocket: pocket which moves with the quarterback.

Free Kick: whenever a team calls a fair catch, it is allowed a free kick where, without interference, it may try to kick a field goal. Also, a free kick is given a team after committing a safety. The ball is punted from the 20-yard line by the team that committed the safety.

Front Four: the 4 members of the defensive line. Famous fronts have included Dallas' *Doomsday Defense*, Minnesota's *Purple People-Eaters* and Pittsburgh's *Steel Curtain*.

Gap 8: an 8-man, goal-line-stand line.

Goal Line Defense: defense, close to a team's own goal line, which uses more men than usual on the line to prevent power thrusts up the middle.

Grind It Out: to move up field with small steady gains.

Hole: spot in the line made vacant by the blockers for the runner to shoot through.

Horn: the referee's whistle.

I-Formation: formation where the offense places two or more backs behind the quarterback in succession, forming an imaginary **I** from the center to the last back. Often employed with tight end in the backfield.

Illegal Motion: back or lineman moving before the ball is snapped and after the team is officially set. A team must come to a full set 1 second before the snap of the ball. Also refers to a back moving forward (toward the line of scrimmage) before the ball is snapped. Legally, he may only run away from or parallel to scrimmage line.

Illegal Receiver: interior lineman who runs downfield.

JOP: acronym for jumping on the pile of tacklers.

Kamikazes: members of the Suicide (special) Teams.

Kicking Tee: small rubber device used for propping the ball up for kickoffs.

Lollipop: soft, hanging pass, easy to intercept.

Man in Motion: method of having a back running to another spot on the field after the team's placement on the line of scrimmage but before snap of the ball.

Monster Man: combination linebacker-defensive back who is allowed to roam freely.

Near Side: television term meaning side closer to the camera.

Neutral Zone: area between the opposing teams on scrimmage line.

Nickel Defense: placing of 1 extra defensive back in the secondary when expecting a pass.

Pass Interference: illegal interference with the receiver's or defender's right to catch the ball.

Penetrating Defense: defense which tries to prevent a gain and to force a loss or mistake on every play. Also refers to the playing of the man instead of the ball.

Piling On: act of jumping on downed men after the whistle is blown.

Pitchout: play where the quarterback, upon immediate reception of the ball, tosses it straight back to a runner, initiating a running play.

Play Action: passing play with the appearance of a run.

Pocket: blocking wall set up to protect the quarterback.

Post Pattern: receiver pattern that extends straight down the field and inward across the middle at a 90-degree angle or less.

Prevent: defense which tries to stop a long pass, employed in situations such as the end of the game, when the losing team is trying to score quickly.

Primary Receiver: receiver who is the basic target in the play.

Terms

Pulling Guards: term referring to the 2 guards who begin a running play or sweep by forming the blocking wall in front of the back.
Pursuit: following of a play, where all members of the defense methodically pursue the ball carrier.
QUAB: acronym for quickness, agility and balance in a player's form.
Quick Release: passing style where the quarterback hits his receiver soon after the snap.
Quick Hitter: running play with little movement crossways in the line. The ball carrier runs straight through a hole vacated by linemen who block hard and fast, trying to sneak the runner past a slower-acting defender.
Roll-out: play where the quarterback circles back to either side, waiting for a pass or running spot to open. He has the option to pass or run.
Running Quarterback: signal caller who is adept at passing and running, and often plans plays around this option. Different from a *scrambler* insofar as the latter runs on instinct only when receivers are covered, not by plan.
Safety: usually occurs when an offensive man is tackled in his own end zone, or when a bad snap on an intended punt floats over the back-end line. Two points are awarded the defensive team.
Safety Blitz: gambling play where the defensive team shoots a safety through the line.
Safety Valve: pass thrown desperately—or sometimes by design—to a running back near the side lines after a deep passing pattern has developed. This can catch the defense napping if they fail to spot the targeted back coming out of the blocking area.
Scrambler: quarterback who intends to pass but is forced out of the pocket by a good rush and prefers to dodge and run until he either finds a receiver or makes a gain.
Screen Pass: deceptive play intended to fool the defense into thinking a deep pass is developing, as blockers let the linemen penetrate deep into the backfield. Meanwhile, a wall of blockers forms for a back, who takes the pass from the quarterback and tries to penetrate a defense which is now left open.
Secondary: defensive backfield, or the zone, which the offense tries to penetrate with a pass.
Secondary Receiver: planned receiver but not the first choice to catch the pass.
Shotgun: formation where the quarterback takes a direct, deep pass from center as he stands as the deepest back.
Side line Pass: receiver's pattern in which he runs straight out then cuts to the side line at a 90-degree angle. Usually thrown to the near side of the field, it is hard to defend and works best to stop the clock.
Sitting on the Ball: act of running the clock out at the end of the game or half. A ploy by the winning team as a defensive tactic to prevent scoring by the opponent.
Slash: block by a wide receiver or linebacker.
Soccer-style Kicker: kicker approaches the ball from an angle and kicks with the side of his foot. (See *Plays & Formations*.)
Strip: to grab or knock the ball from the carrier.
Strong Right or Left Side: side with the tight end. Announcers will indicate as the offense sets up.
Strong Safety: safety who plays the offense's strong side, usually covering the tight end.
Stunting: defensive ploy, moving linebackers or sending linemen off to different angles to confuse the defenders.
Stutter Step: shuffling or stepping the feet quickly to give the appearance that the receiver is going to cut or stop. Meant to shake or dazzle the defense.
Sudden Death or Sudden Life: rare occurrence, applying only to a title game in which the game is tied at the end of regulation play. The first team to score wins, often by a field goal.
Suicide Squad: group of second stringers and rookies used only on kickoffs, punts and place kicks. The idea is that a regular player risks too much from an injury that could occur from the prevalent downfield blocking on these plays.
Sweep: running play which carries the ball to the outside rather than through the line.
Swing Pass: pass thrown immediately out to the side, hitting a back.
Touchback: often mistakenly referred to when a safety occurs. It is the purposeful downing of the ball by a team in their own end zone. Occurs on punts and kickoffs.
Traffic: flow of blockers, the ball-carrier and the gathering tacklers.
Trap: play where the offense lures a defender across the line, or fakes a linebacker out of position, and catches him with a block coming at his blind side (from behind), leaving a big hole to run through.
Turnover: change of ball possession caused by an error rather than by a kick or by one team running out of downs. Fumbles and interceptions are turnovers.
Two-minute Warning: period when the clock is stopped with 2 minutes left in the half or the game. All stadium clocks are now official.
Weak Safety: safety who plays the weak side of the offense. Also called *free safety* because he is free to play the ball or his choice of men.
Weak Side: the side of the offense opposite the tight end.
X: the split end.
Y: the tight end
Z: the wide receiver (flankerback).
Zone: a pass defense where a receiver is picked up only when he enters a certain defender's territory.

When does a team consist of 12 players, not 11? This happens in the Canadian Football League. The twelfth man is called a *flying wing* and may play either in the backfield or line. Where does a first down need to be accomplished in 3 tries and not 4? Again, in Canadian pro ball, where you get just 3 shots to gain 10 yards.

The New York Sack Exchange is the nickname of the New York Jets' defensive line, which in 1981 sacked quarterbacks 66 times—one short of the NFL record set by the Oakland Raiders of 1967. **Joe Klecko**, the Sack Exchange's leader, led the league in this department last season with 20½ sacks. (He shared in one sacking).

How often do visiting pro teams win? In 1980, it was 45% of games; in 1981, it fell to 37.7%, indicating that travel can be injurious to health and performance.

Major upset of 1981: the feared Oakland Raiders, defending their NFL championship, lost 3 straight games by shutouts—to teams that didn't make the Super Bowl playoffs. This was the first time an NFL team was unable to score in 3 consecutive starts since 1943. The Raiders finished the year with a lowly 7-9 record.

One veteran NFL referee described his duties as "...trying to maintain order during a legalized gang brawl involving 80 toughs with a little whistle, a hanky and a ton of prayer."

Pro officials are known as *zebras* (for their striped shirts) and *The Seven Blind Mice* by fans, who boo them a lot. The whistle-tooters refer to themselves, with pride, as *the third team on the field.*

The Job: To travel more than 125,000 miles per year on 20 weekends and enforce more than 1,800 rules in a book running to 210 pages.

The pay: First or 2nd year NFL officials each receive $325 for regular season games; veteran officials receive $850 per regular season game; $1,500 is the remuneration for divisional playoffs. The Super Bowl is worth $3,000 per man.

Who Does It: NFL Supervisor of Officials Art McNally's roster of 105 referees, umpires and others is made up of self-trained experts from all walks: teachers, engineers, athletic directors, policemen, lawyers, sports-goods salesmen, physicians and bankers. A few are believed to be millionaires, owning their own companies. For most, it is a labor of love, a fascinating sideline.

Oddly, only a dozen of the current 105 registered officials are former NFL players. Best-known of the ex-players is **Pat Harder**, one-time All-Pro back with the Detroit Lions and the Chicago Cardinals, now an auto company vice president. Oldest official in terms of years of service is **Lou Palazzi**, an ex-New York Giants center, with 30 seasons of officiating. Palazzi is a landscape architect.

Most famous of the 105 are: **Pat Haggerty**, (wearing No. 4 on his shirt), an aggressive, take-charge type who refereed the 1982 Super Bowl; and **Jim Tunney**, (No. 3), a tall, tough, Gary Cooper-type referee with 22 years in the league. Haggerty is a Colorado State U teacher-coach. Tunney heads his own California motivation company.

Breakdown of officials. Seven men are needed to run a Pro game. Until 1929, the NFL made do with 3 officials. In that year, a fourth *tooter* was added (field judge). In 1947 a fifth was added (back judge). In 1965 came a sixth (line judge). Finally, in 1977, a seventh official was named (side judge). Their duties:

1 **Referee:** charged with general oversight and control of the game. Signals all fouls and is final authority on rules interpretation. Positioned 10-12 yards behind the scrimmage line, he keys on the quarterback for violations, fumbles, etc. Observes punter similarly. Can eject any player or slap a 15-yard penalty on a player or coach guilty of unsportsmanlike conduct.

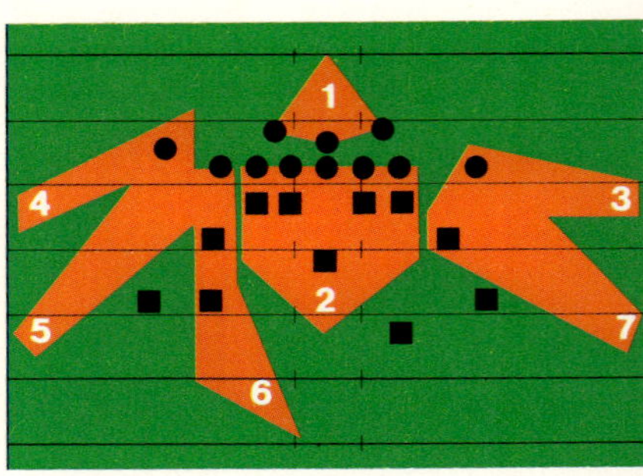

2 **Umpire:** primary responsibility is to rule on players' equipment, false starts at scrimmage, legality of offensive line blocking and of defensive counters to blocking. Stands 4-5 yards downfield behind linebackers.

3 **Head linesman:** chiefly responsible for ruling on pre-snap encroachment at the scrimmage line, side line plays on his side, keeping track of downs and supervising the side line chain crew.

4 **Line judge:** straddling scrimmage line on the field opposite the Head Linesman, he keeps time of the game as backup to the clock operator. Also observes wide receivers on his side, legality of pass and flight of ball on pass.

5 **Back judge:** operates on the same side of field as the Line Judge, 15-17 yards deep. Keys on tight end and nearest back. Rules from deep position on holding or illegal use of hands by defensive men, pass interference and out-of-bounds situations in his area.

6 **Field judge:** positioned 22-25 yards downfield, he keys on the tight end and near back. Watches for blocking violations, rules on holding or illegal hand usage by receivers or defenders. He times the 30-second interval between plays, the intermission and the pause between the 2 periods of each half. Rules on success or failure of field goals.

7 **Side judge:** has multiple duties, overlapping those of other judges. Also rules on loose-ball activity and calls clipping on punt returns.
(College football uses 6 officials, whose duties largely are the same as those of pro officials.)

Oddball feat: QB **Bobby Douglas** of the Chicago Bears scored 4 touchdowns on November 4, 1973 and ran only 15 feet in doing it. Douglas had 3 plunges of 1 yard and a 2-yarder.

Equipment. On freezing-weather days, officials wear thermal underwear under plastic suits, a ski jacket under the uniform shirt, earmuffs and gloves. Still, they suffer frostbite. Umpire **Joe Connell** once blew his whistle in zero weather and part of his lip came away with the whistle.

A rubber band, moved from finger to finger, is used by some referees as a supplemental means of keeping track of downs.

The *Little Thunderer®* whistle (very loud) is preferred by referees.

Will videotape become an officiating aid? Fans demand it—don't get it. Electronic aids for calling such close plays as side line pass-catches appear unlikely in the near future. NFL owners oppose using TV's instant-replay, or *second look*, for these reasons: (1) it would require 12 cameras to cover all angles of a play, an impractical number; (2) an eighth official would be needed to evaluate replays; (3) coaches' demand for TV-replay of disputed plays would cause horrendous delays.

The NFL states that officials have been proven correct in 98 per cent of all rulings and that it is best to keep the game in human hands. Many fans disagree. They argue that 2 per cent of incorrect calls can cost a team a conference title or Super Bowl berth—and probably has done so in the past.

Funniest officiating sight. Before 85,000 at Berkeley, Cal., Referee Tom Louttit and his crew chased a loose dog about the field for 10 minutes and failed to capture him. Then the dog turned on Louttit and bit him. Then he attacked the other whistle-tooters and put everyone to flight.

The game is simple in objective: to move the other 11 gents out of your way.

Whichever team consistently hits hardest—knocking down or otherwise foiling the most defenders—usually walks away the victor.

But rules must exist to govern 22 men in a Pier-6 brawl. And here it gets complicated. The pros and collegians, in some cases, do not march to the same battle code. Additionally, both factions have hundreds of sections, articles, sub-articles and exceptions in their rules books.

Fans don't need to know it all. The basics and a bit more are sufficient.

Scoring

Scoring can happen in 1 of 4 ways:

1. **Touchdown** (6 points): Above the goal line is an imaginary vertical plane, extending from the ground to infinity. The *goal line* is inside and part of the *end zone*, **not** part of the 100-yard playing field. If the ball crosses that plane by any discernable fraction of an inch, it's a touchdown. TDs also can be scored by catching a legal pass in the end zone, recovering an offensive team's fumble in that team's end zone, or by recovering a ball kicked into an end zone that's been touched by a member of the receiving team.
2. **Field goal** (3 points): May be tried from any yard line. The ball must pass between the goal post uprights (see *NFL-NCAA Rule Differences*) and over a crossbar 10 feet from the ground. A dropkick may be used, but isn't—it's done by placement, employing a holder and a kicker.
3. **Point-after-touchdown** (1 or 2 points—see *NCAA/NFL Rule Differences*): A little bonus for scoring a touchdown, the PAT must be kicked from scrimmage, anywhere between the inbound lines. The defensive team *never* can score on a point-after attempt that's short or blocked. Ball is dead.
4. **Safety** (2 points): The key factor in a safety is *impetus*. Two points go to Team A when the ball is dead on or behind Team B's goal line if the impetus that put the ball there came from Team B. **Example A:** A QB or runner retreats into his end zone—providing the impetus himself—and is downed there. **Example B:** On a pass-interception, a player goes into his own end zone and is downed. This is *not* a safety, but a *touchback* (no points), because the impetus came from the passing team. (Often confused with a safety, it occurs when the ball is dead on or behind a team's goal line if the *impetus came from an opponent* and provided it is not a touchdown or missed field goal.)

Lineup

Lineup at scrimmage. With 11 men on each side, the offensive team must have 7 men on the scrimmage line at the snap of the ball. Other rules include:

Players not on the scrimmage line must be at least *1 yard* behind the others at the snap of the ball.
All offensive team players must be *stationary* except *1 back*, who may be in motion parallel to the scrimmage line, or backward, (but *not* forward).
After a shift or huddle, all offensive team players must be set—at an absolute stop for at least *1 second*, with no movement of body parts to draw an opponent offside.
The defensive team may deploy itself as it wishes, so long as it does not encroach on the *neutral zone*. The neutral zone is defined as a space the length of the football between the 2 lines of scrimmagers.
Encroachment occurs when a player (a) moves into the neutral zone at time of the snap, or (b) makes contact with an opponent before the snap. *Penalty: 5 yards.*

Kickoff

Kickoff is a long boot accompanied by an 11-man charge downfield at the start of each half and after a field goal and point-after-touchdown attempt (PAT). A punt may be used on the kickoff, but you rarely see it anymore. Other facts you should know about kickoffs:

- The other 10 players must be **behind the kicker** when he boots the ball from the 35 or 40-yard line (see *NFL-NCAA Rules Differences*)
- A kicking tee **up to 3"** high may be used.
- A kickoff is legal only after the ball **travels** 10 yards or is **touched** by the receiving team. If touched, it's a free ball—up for grabs.
- When a kickoff goes out of bounds without being touched by the receiving team, it must be **kicked again**—with a *5-yard penalty*.
- If a kickoff goes through an opponent's goal post, it's not a field goal (some argue that such a feat should be rewarded with 3 points).

Downs

Downs: The system whereby a team must gain **10 yards** within 4 attempts (downs) was the invention of **Walter *Father of Football* Camp** in the 1880s. As late as 1912, only 5 yards gained in 3 tries was needed to retain possession of the ball. Today, a 10-yard pickup within 4 downs means that a team retains possession for another series of 4 downs. If, after 3 downs, a team is well short of the needed 10 yards, a final-down punt usually is in order. But teams often gamble and go for the *first and 10* (See *Plays & Formations*).

Passing

Forward pass rules vary slightly between the pro and college game. Keep these in mind:

- A forward pass may be touched or caught by any eligible receiver. All members of the defensive team are eligible. Eligible receivers on the offensive team are players on either end of the line (other than center, guard or tackle) or players at least one yard behind the line at the snap. A T-formation quarterback is **not** eligible to receive a forward pass during a play from scrimmage. **Exception**—T-formation quarterback becomes eligible if pass is previously touched by an eligible receiver.
- An offensive team may make only **1** forward pass during each play from scrimmage. *Penalty: loss of down.*
- The passer must be behind his line of scrimmage. *Penalty: loss of down and 5 yards, enforced from the spot of pass.*
- Any **eligible offensive player** may catch a forward pass. If a pass is touched by one offensive player and then **touched or caught by a second eligible offensive player**, pass completion is legal. Further, all offensive players become eligible **once a pass is touched** by an eligible receiver or any defensive player.

Forward pass/ineligible receiver penalties:

- If the ball is touched *accidentally* or caught by an ineligible receiver **on or behind his line.** *Penalty: loss of down.*
- If ineligible receiver is **illegally downfield.** *Penalty: 10 yards.*
- If touched or caught (intentionally or accidentally) by ineligible receiver **beyond** the line. *Penalty: loss of 10 yards.*
- If ineligible receiver is **illegally downfield.** *Penalty: 10 yards.*

If a forward pass is caught **simultaneously** by eligible players on *opposing teams*, possession goes to the **passing** team.

Any forward pass becomes incomplete and the ball is dead if:

- Pass **hits the ground** or goes **out-of-bounds.**
- It **hits the goal post** or the crossbar of either team.
- It is caught by an offensive player after **touching an ineligible receiver.**
- An illegal pass is **caught by the passer.**

A forward pass is complete when an eligible receiver touches the ground with **both feet** inbounds while **in possession** of the ball. If a receiver is carried out-of-bounds by an opponent while in possession in the air, the pass is complete **at the spot where the receiver went out-of-bounds.**

If an eligible receiver goes out-of-bounds **accidentally** or is **forced out** by a defender and **returns** to catch a pass, the play is regarded as a pass caught out-of-bounds. *Penalty: loss of down, no yardage.*

On a **fourth down pass**—when the offensive team is *inside* the opposition's 20-yard line—an incomplete pass in the field of play or in the end zone results in a loss of down **at the line of scrimmage.**

If a personal foul is committed by the **defense** *prior to* the completion of a pass, the *penalty is 15 yards* **from the spot where the ball becomes dead.**

If a **personal foul** is committed by the **defense** *prior to* the completion of a pass, the *penalty is 15 yards* **from the spot where the ball becomes dead.**

If a **personal foul** is committed by the **offense** *prior to* the completion of a pass, the *penalty is 15 yards* **from the previous line of scrimmage.**

Intentional grounding of a forward pass is a foul. *Penalty: loss of down and 10-yard penalty from the line of scrimmage if passer is in the field of play, or; loss of down where the foul occured if it occured more than 10 yards behind the line of scrimmage, or; safety if passer is in his own end zone when ball is released.*

It is considered intentional grounding of a forward pass when the ball strikes the ground after the passer throws, tosses or lobs the ball to prevent a loss of yardage by his team.

Rules protecting passer: Until 1979, tacklers with an almost unimpeded shot at pro quarterbacks laid many of these priceless properties in hospitals. Then came the **quick whistle rule** which states, "Officials are to blow the play dead as soon as the QB is clearly in the

grasp and control of any tackler.'' In 1980, this restriction was expanded to read ''...in the grasp and control anywhere behind the scrimmage line.'' The rule remains hotly opposed by those arguing that the QB is overly shielded. Also, what referee can precisely say when the QB is ''under control'' and can't wiggle loose? The philosophy of college football is quite different. (See *NFL-NCAA Rule Differences*).

Pass interference: This is another judgmental matter which annually causes great uproar. The NFL rule says, It is interference when any player's movement hinders the progress of an opponent in his attempt to reach a pass. **Exception:** Such incidental movement or contact when 2 or more players make a *simultaneous* and *bona fide* attempt to catch or bat the ball, is permitted.'' A *simultaneous* and *bona fide* attempt means each player is playing the ball and contact is unavoidable. The NCAA generally agrees with this interpretation.

In the pros, a pass begins when the QB **brings his hand forward.** He can't be legally hit **once the ball leaves his hand.** The referee has the tough task of determining whether a tackler had a *reasonable chance* to stop his momentum.

Fumbles

Fumble: Fans should learn to distinguish between a *fumble* and a *muff*. A fumble is loss of possession of the ball. A muff is the touching of a loose ball by a player in an unsuccessful attempt to gain possession. A fumble may be advanced by any player on either team regardless of whether he recovers the ball before or after it hits the turf.

Fair catch: This is the catch of a kick by a receiver in which he extends 1 arm upward while the ball is in the air—and thus can neither run with (return) the kick or be tackled after the catch. It's a *quid pro quo* situation. A *fair-catcher* is not required to catch the ball. He can abort his mission if he so desires.

Penalties

Automatic first down awarded to offensive team on *all defensive fouls* with these exceptions:

- •Offside
- •Encroachment
- •Delay of game
- •Illegal substitution
- •Excessive time-out(s)

Loss of down (no yardage)

- •Second forward pass *behind* the line
- Forward pass strikes ground, goal post or crossbar
- •Forward pass goes out-of-bounds
- •Forward pass is first touched by eligible receiver who has gone out-of-bounds and returned
- •Forward pass touches or is caught by an ineligible receiver on or behind the line
- •Forward pass thrown from behind line of scrimmage after ball once crossed the line.

Five yards

- •Crawling
- •Defensive holding or illegal use of hands (automatic first down)
- •Delay of game
- •Encroachment
- •Too many time-outs
- •False start
- •Illegal formation
- •Illegal shift
- •Illegal motion
- •Illegal substitution
- •Kickoff out-of-bounds between goal lines and not touched
- •Invalid fair catch signal
- •More than 11 players on the field at snap for either team
- •Less than 7 men on offensive line at snap
- •Offside
- •Failure to pause 1 second after shift or huddle
- •Running into kicker (automatic first down)
- •More than 1 man in motion at snap
- •Grasping face mask of opponent (if by defense, automatic first down)
- •Player out-of-bounds at snap
- •Ineligible member(s) of kicking team going beyond line of scrimmage before ball is kicked
- •Illegal return
- •Failure to report change of eligibility

Five yards and loss of down

- •Forward pass thrown from *beyond line of scrimmage*

Ten yards

- •Offensive pass interference
- •Ineligible player downfield during passing down
- •Holding, illegal use of hands, arms or body by offense
- •Tripping by a member of either team
- •Helping the runner

Ten yards and loss of down

- •Intentional grounding of forward pass (safety if passer is in own end zone). If foul occurs more than 10 yards behind the line, play results in a loss of down at spot of foul.

Fifteen yards

- •Clipping below the waist
- •Fair catch interference
- •Illegal batting or punching loose ball
- •Deliberately kicking a loose ball
- •Illegal crackback block by offense
- •Piling on (automatic first down)
- •Roughing the kicker (automatic first down)
- •Roughing the passer (automatic first down)
- •Twisting, turning or pulling an opponent by the face mask
- •Unnecessary roughness
- •Unsportsmanlike conduct
- •Delay of game at start of either half
- •Illegal blocking below the waist
- •A tackler using his helmet to butt, spear or ram an opponent
- •Any player who uses the top of his helmet unnecessarily

Fifteen yards (and disqualification if flagrant)

- •Striking an opponent with fist
- •Kicking or kneeing an opponent
- •Striking opponent to head or neck with forearm, elbow or hands—whether or not the initial contact is made below the neck area
- •Roughing kicker
- •Roughing passer
- •Malicious unnecessary roughness
- •Unsportsmanlike conduct
- •Palpably unfair act (*distance penalty determined by the referee after consultation with other officials*)

Fifteen yards and loss of coin toss option

- •Team's late arrival on the field prior to scheduled kickoff

Major differences between NFL and NCAA rules. If you switch from a televised college game on Saturday (sis-rah-boom!) to a Sunday pro contest (highly analyzed by such commentators as John Madden, Hank Stram or John Brodie), it will help to know that:

- To promote more and longer kickoff returns, the pros kick off from the 35-yard line. Colleges kick from the 40-yard line.
- On point-after-touchdown attempts, the colleges get 1 point for kicking the ball through the posts, 2 points for running or passing it over the goal line. The option is available. In the NFL, there's only the 1-point kick—there is no option.
- The pro ball is all leather; colleges can use a rubber or composition-cover ball if agreed upon beforehand. Only the college ball has white stripes (2).
- Colleges are not so gung-ho about protecting the quarterback-passer. They blow the whistle only when the passer is *down or stopped*, often meaning he takes a beating. The **quick whistle** rule is observed in the NFL.
- Five to 6 officials work college games; the NFL uses 7.
- The college goal post width between uprights is 23′4″, almost 5 feet wider than the pros' 18′6″.
- When a college game ends after 4 periods in a tie score, it's a tie forever. In the NFL, a *sudden death* overtime period of 15 minutes is provided. Whichever team scores first is the winner. That goes for all games except the playoffs and Super Bowl. In the latter cases, teams continue to play as many overtime periods as are necessary to break the tie and determine a winner.
- Colleges spot the ball for the conversion attempt at the 3-yard line, while the NFL spots it on the 2-yard line.
- The college rule on fumbles is that when a fumble touches the ground, only the team that has fumbled can advance the ball. In the NFL, a fumble may be picked up and advanced by any player on either team. If the fumble is caught in the air, both the NFL and NCAA permit either team to advance the ball.
- Holding an opponent (that demon violation) costs a *10-yard penalty* in college play, *15 yards* in the pro game.
- A receiver in college needs to have just 1 foot inbounds at the time of the catch, ''...if he has possession and control of the ball.'' The pros require both feet to be inbounds ''...while in possession.''
- A pro running back or receiver, with the ball, may continue to run after he slips to the ground without being tackled. In the NCAA, the runner may not advance if any part of his body except his hands and feet touch the ground.
- Missed field goals in the NFL result in the ball being returned to the point where the kick was made (line of scrimmage) or to the 20-yard line, whichever is farther from the goal line. Colleges spot missed FGs at the 20-yard line. *Note:* This makes a long FG try much more of a gamble in the NFL.
- Colleges may suit up as many men as they like for a home game, 90 or more, and travel with 60 or even more players. NFL squad limit is 45 at all times.

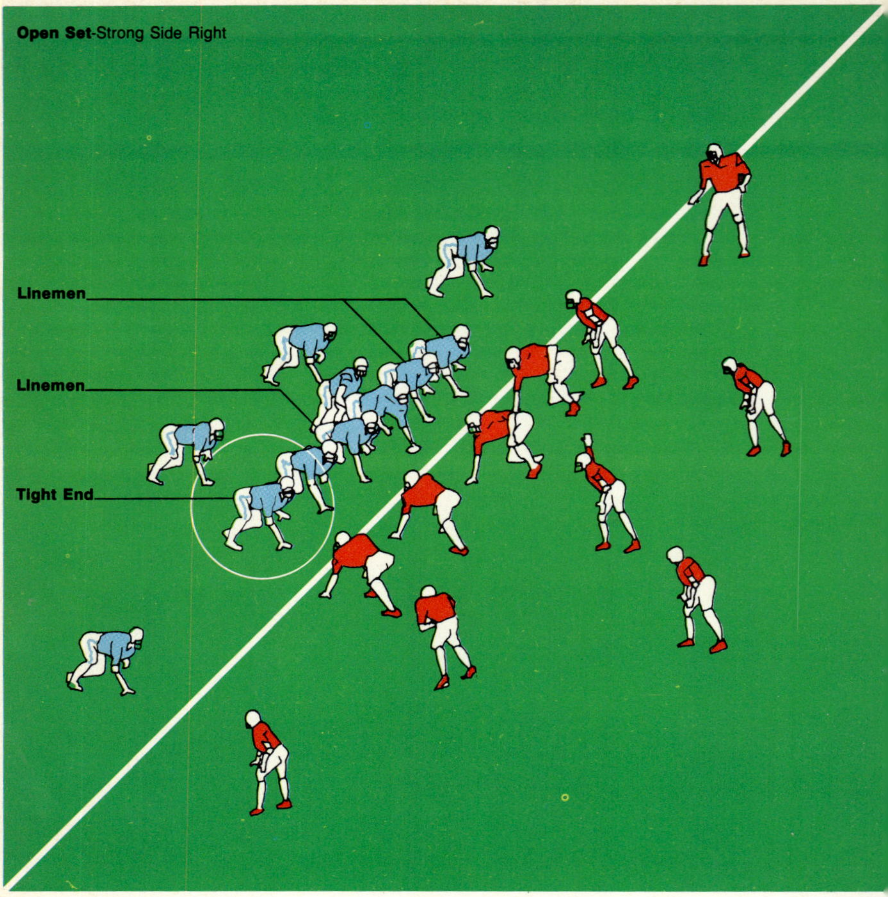

Open Set-Strong Side Right

Linemen

Linemen

Tight End

"Getting there fastest with the mostest"—as a Civil War general phrased it—governs how pro teams line up following the kickoff. Imbalance and sowing confusion is the name of the game.

As shown in this sketch, teams usually attack off either a **strong** side or a **weak** side. The positioning of the **tight end** usually decides which side is strong. Joining him to the right or left is the **wide receiver** (also known as the **flankerback**), so that 2 receivers and 2 linemen (**guard** and **tackle**) are stationed on one side (the strong side), and only 1 receiver and 2 linemen on the weak side.

As a matter of general practice, a strong side **right** lineup is preferred. Football is a right-handed game mainly because quarterbacks, the most important individuals, almost always are right-handers and work more naturally in that direction.

But many switcheroos can come off either strong or weak sides. This is why a defense, well-balanced at the start, stays loose—ready to spring into action and adjust in any direction the moment it smells a play in advance or *reads* a developing one.

All offensive play starts from a formation—or, in the lingo of coaches, a **set**. But sets differ in purpose. Some are designed to connect on a pass to a hopefully unprotected spot, others to earn yardage via a run. Still others provide the quarterback with an option—to pass, to run, or to keep the ball himself to advance. The option chosen depends upon how the play develops and it must be decided in seconds.

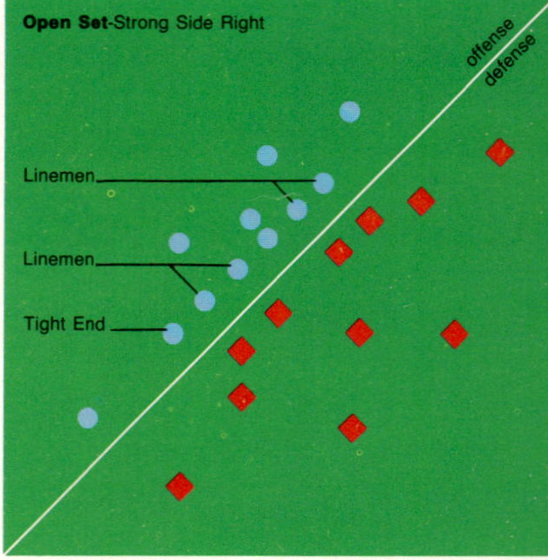

One of the common, bread-and-butter professional formations is the **Open Set**, or **Pro-T.** As part of a 7-man line, the **tight end** is set close to the tackle. A **wide receiver** or flankerback is positioned wide left, behind the tight end. A **split end** is stationed wide to the right. The **quarterback** is over the center, with 2 **running backs** on either side of him and 3-5 yards to his rear. The split end and tight end may take their stance on either side of the line, depending on where the attack will strike.

The **Open Set** has power and versatility. The **split end, tight end** or **wide receiver** can become pass-receivers. Or, either of the **running backs** can take a handoff and crack into the line or elsewhere.

Plays off Open or Pro-T Set. Typical of an **Open Set** play is the **tackle slant**. Whirling at the snap, the **QB** jams the ball into an **RB's** belly. After crossing behind the **QB** to take the handoff, the **RB** zeroes in on a space between his **left tackle** and **tight end.** The 2 key blocks are:
1. by the **tight end** on the **defensive end**, and
2. by the other **running back** on the **linebacker**. Meanwhile, the wide receiver at the far left fakes going out for a pass to decoy the **cornerback**.

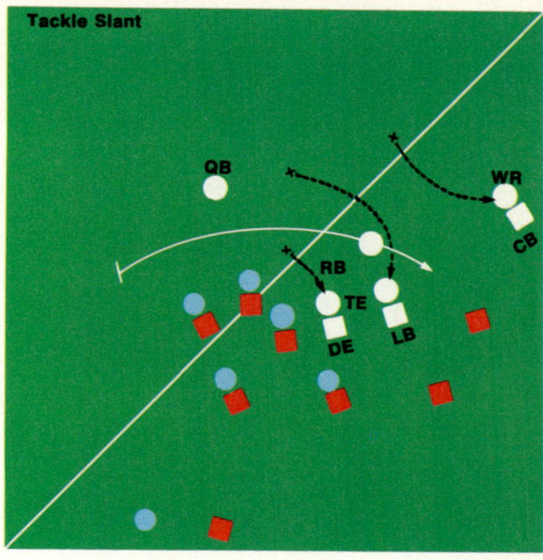

Tackle Slant-Off Open Set

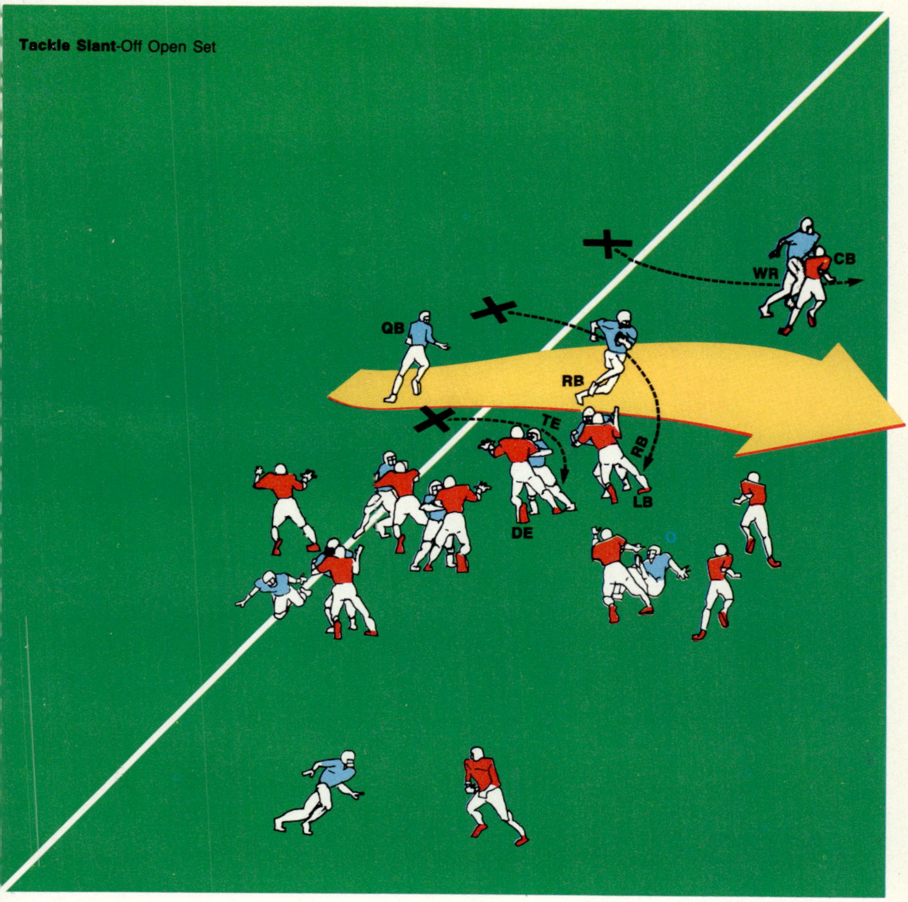

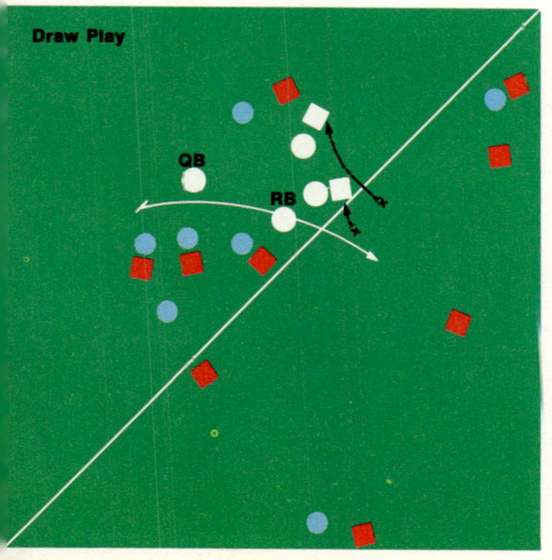

Another maneuver off the **Open Set** is the ordinary **line buck**. Here the **RB** hits between his **center** and **guard**, who block to the outside momentarily to open a hole. The **RB** must get to this opening—*fast*.

Still another tactic is the **draw play**. Linemen check up as if protecting on a pass. The defense goes for the gag and charges in to mug the **QB.** But he's slipped the ball to an **RB**, who shoots past the incoming, gung-ho defenders for a good gain. **Trap plays** similarly are based on fakery, with a particular lineman allowed free access to the backfield. Whereupon, *whap!*—he's blocked to one side.

The **sweep** (*student body right*) is an end run in which both **guards** pull out, dash down the scrimmage line and, along with a big blocking **back,** wipe out tacklers. This is a nifty power play *if* the ball-carrier is able to go from a lateral route to turning the corner and heading downfield. (This is seldom used because **cornerbacks** and outside **linebackers** have a way of anticipating it in advance).

The thrilling **Statue of Liberty** stunt has all but vanished. Too obvious. But an offshot of it, the **Reverse End-around**, is popular. The play begins like a sweep, but then the **split end** comes from the opposite direction of the flow to snatch the ball from the **QB** and head for daylight. In the **Double Reverse**, all hell breaks loose. The ball is swiftly exchanged from the **QB** to the **flankerback** running left, to the **RB,** going right (or vice versa). This isn't often used because cornerbacks and wide linebackers have a cute way of anticipating it.

From the **Open Set**, the fundamental formation, coaching master-minds branch out in all directions. They line up in a wide variety of formations: **multiple sets.** They change **blocking patterns.** They use **shifts** and **men-in-motion** all with one purpose: to dazzle the defense and prevent it from gaining a clear idea of what's coming at them. The more different *looks* an offense presents to a defense, the more confusion can be sown.

Four main steps are involved in putting a pass on the money to a receiver:

1. The **QB**, having called the play in the huddle, crouches over his **center's** buttocks. He uses a nonrhythmic cadence count of signals, a combination of coded sounds aimed at mystifying the other guys, perhaps even pulling them offside for a penalty. Hidden somewhere in his chatter is the specific play-call.

2. The **center's** snap delivers the ball to the **QB's** hands, which are forked: right hand on top, left hand below in a cup. The ball is transferred with the laces along the second joint of the **QB's** fingers, already in throwing position.

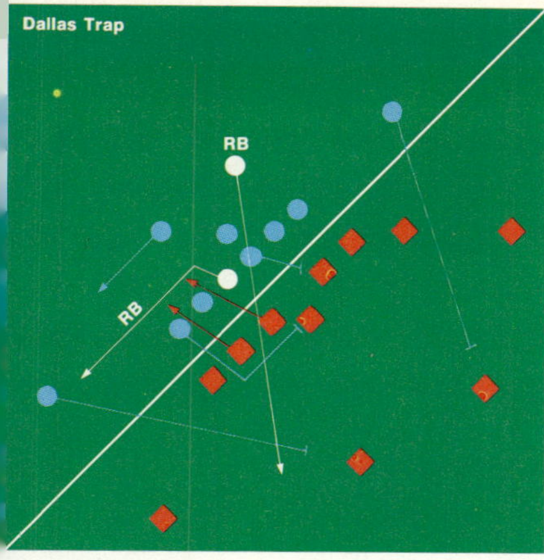

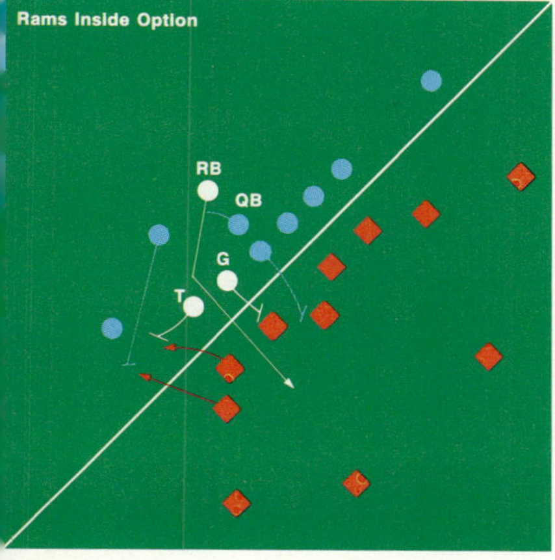

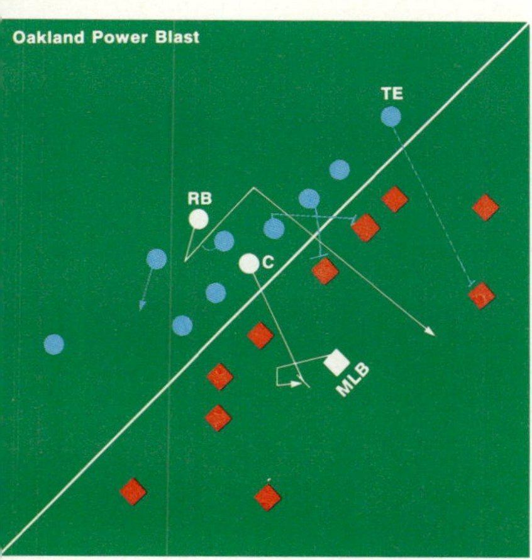

Plays & Formations

The following illustrates how this works on ground plays:

Dallas Cowboys' Influence Trap: This is an **Open Set** variation. The **right guard** pulls to his right as if leading a play in that direction. This influences the key **defensive tackle** to chase him. As the tackle follows, the **left guard** trap-blocks him, and the play turns out to be Running Back **Tony Dorsett** diving up the middle through the tackle's vacated space.

Rams' Inside Option: An option running play in which the **defensive end** is the designated sap. The **running back** starts outside, causing the protecting end to move in that direction. The **tight end** blocker nudges the **DE** further to the outside, at which point a running back cuts back and takes the inside option for a chunk of yardage.

Oakland Raiders' Power Blast Left: Sucker them, then flatten them—that's the motto of the Raiders, 3-time Super Bowl finalists. Here they work on the **middle linebacker.** The **fullback**, handed the ball, takes a stutter step to his right, suckering the linebacker into starting that way. Then he swerves left between cross-blocking by his **left guard** and **tackle.**

Passing tactics: Aerial warfare—from the short, zipped pass *under* (or inside) the linebackers to the soaring missile called *The Bomb*—delights the public most. *Putting up the ball* has become high-tech art. Quarterbacks tossing 25-30 touchdowns per season are even bigger heroes than home-run sluggers in baseball or 7-foot funky-dunkers in basketball. They take a perpetual beating in the act of throwing, which is why the small, 6-feet or under QB is becoming extinct. The successful field generals stand 6'3" to 6'5" and weigh 210 to 225, such as **Dan Fouts** (San Diego), **Randy White** (Dallas), **Terry Bradshaw** (Pittsburgh) and **Ken Anderson** (Cincinnati). Most have *cat eyes* capable of seeing in 4 or 5 directions at split second intervals.

3. Gripping the ball across the laces, the **QB,** on a drop-back pass, swiftly retreats 6-7 yards. In retreating, he never completely turns his back on the defense. He quick-steps back in a three-quarter-turn position, which enables him to see defensive changes taking place. A semi-circular *pass pocket* forms around him (Secret Service agents have learned from it). In this mode, linemen block at scrimmage and backs not involved as receivers or decoys take the outside linebackers. Depending on how well the pocket stands up, the **QB** can (a) stay with it (b) move up a few steps to let tacklers overrun him (c) scramble to the outside.

4. With ball cocked at shoulder height, the **QB** checks on what the defensive players are doing—*rather* than first looking at his *receivers*. He *knows* where the receivers are going; those covering them are of primary importance. As he delivers the ball, the **QB** strides forward with a strong leg push to provide zip in the exact direction of his target, for accuracy. He is cautious not to eyeball the selected receiver until the last moment. He tips off nothing.

Play-action pass: Designed to get you a passing gain when the situation appears to call for a run, the play-action begins with a spurious run to which the defense may commit itself. The **QB** might fake a flip or handoff to a **running back**, drop back with the ball concealed behind his hip and then unload to the **tight end** downfield. Blocking simulates a line plunge.

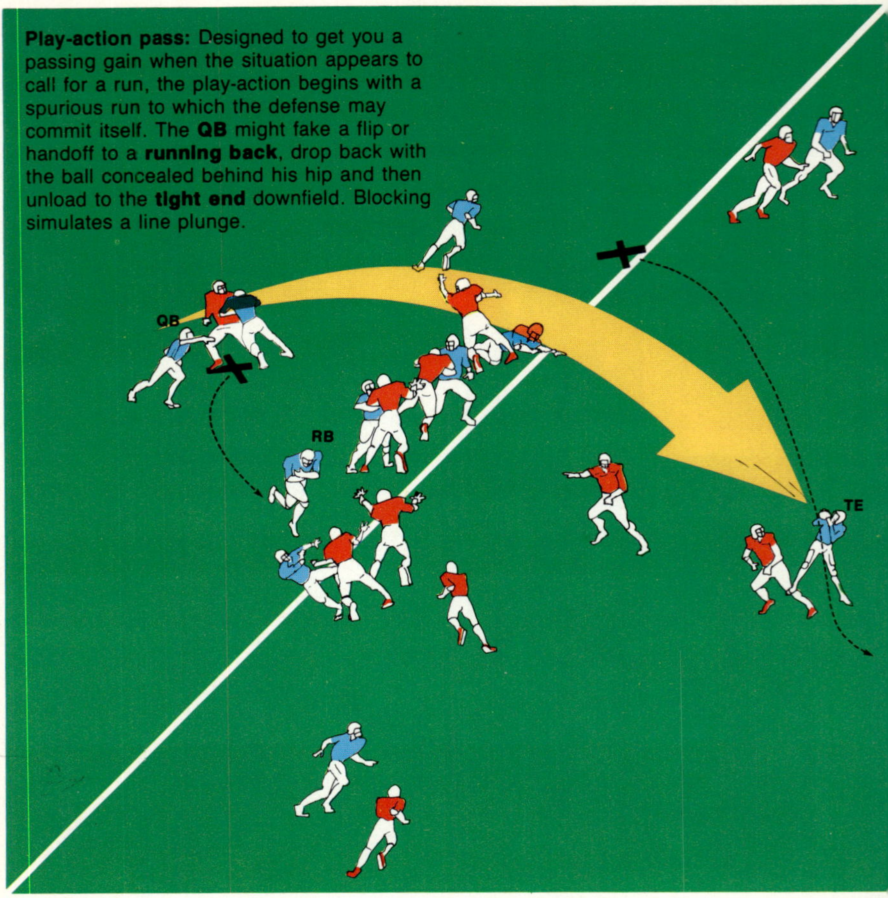

Flag, Post and Flare patterns: The **Flag** route makes the crowd scream—a Bomb-type pass thrown to the end zone corner flag. Amazing catches—and acrobatic interceptions—result. Often the ball is lofted and the **flankerback** runs under it. A play where *interference* debates rage.

The **Post** resembles a Flag, but the **receiver** switches his route and heads toward the goal post. In the **Flare**, a quickie pass is hurled to a **back** flaring out without deception. A short-yardage gainer, but fairly reliable if key blocks are laid on.

PASS ROUTE TREES

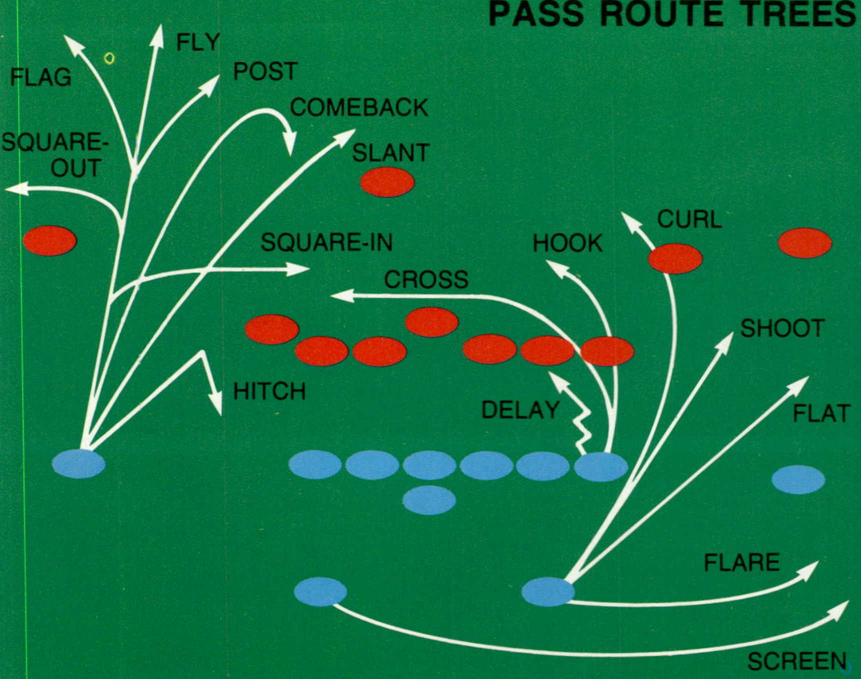

hotgun formation: This **QB** positioning ıys the passer an extra 1½ to 2 seconds ' time to throw. At a signal given during his ıdence-count, the **QB** retreats from the ənter for 4-6 yards and stands there while ɔntinuing the count. From this deep spot, e has a wide-angle, better view of the ıemy's deployment and reaction than the -formation **QB**. Furthermore, he needn't ıke his eyes off the defense while ·treating—he's already there. The Dallas owboys introduced the **Shotgun** with oger Staubach as the passer in 1971. Now 's widely copied in situations where a pass essential and obvious. **Receivers** and **lockers** are widely spread, sometimes :retching almost from side line to side line.

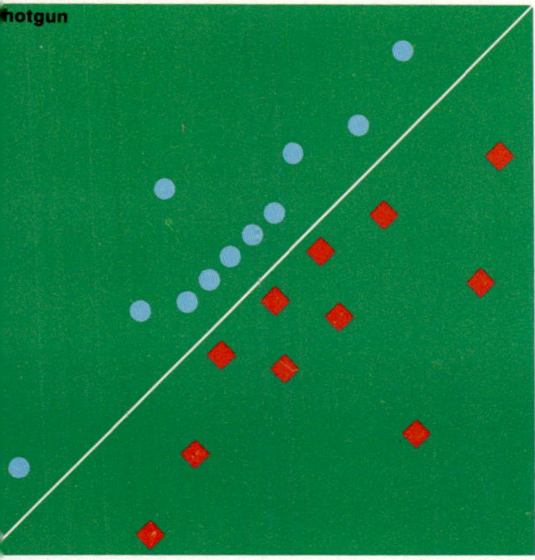

creen pass: You'll see this one used time ıd again. Like no other pass, it speedily ıifts the action from Point **A** (scrum line) to oint **B** (the outside). **Linemen** move over form a wall of interference for a **running ack** who takes a medium-short, well-timed ass from the **QB** and gets behind the :reen.

he passing pocket: Against a 5-man ısh, the normal blocking is as shown. gainst a *red-dog* (2 or 3 linebackers or ɔrnermen rushing) or a *blitz* (3 or more ıen from the defensive secondary coming), lack of enough pocket protection can ıean the **QB** is dumped. *Mad-Dog* means ıat everyone available—such as 3 ıebackers plus others—rushes.

Crossing patterns: There's an infinite number of crosses in any coach's playbook. In this **split end-tight end** combination, the 2 **receivers** run a straight route, then veer to cross each other's paths. The **QB** must decide—which one is the better target of opportunity? **Triple crosses**, using 3 **catchers**, are the toughest to defend.

Flooding a zone: In a **zone defense**, as opposed to **man-to-man**, defenders are assigned a specific territory and they guard it like U.S. Marines. One diabolical way of beating the zone is to send 2 or more ballhawks into the same area, overwhelming the lone sentry. Below, we see 3 receivers each running a different pattern to the same side. A *hitch* or comeback is performed by the **wide receiver** in the end zone, the **running back** flares and the **tight end** does a down-and-out to the sideline. The man who has gone long to the end zone will often pull the defender after him, leaving the other 2 open for a pass at the 5 or 15-yardline.

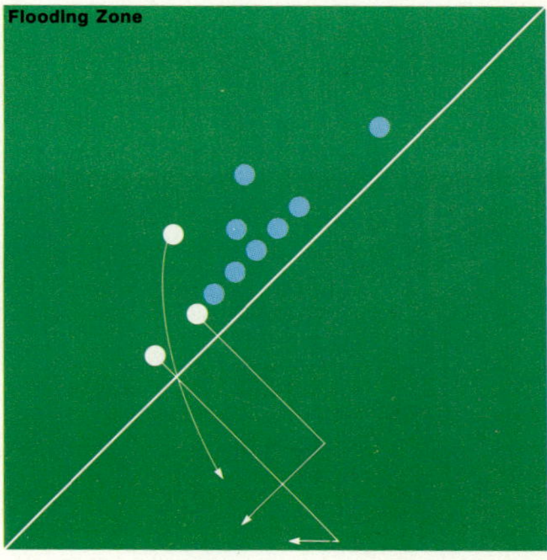

College football offenses: Since *amateur* school ball is distinctly different from that played by the mercenaries, collegiate formations and plays have their own flavor. A handful of colleges use the **Pro Set.** But, led by coaches **Barry Switzer** (Oklahoma), **Tom Osborne** (Nebraska), *Bear* **Bryant** (Alabama) and **Vince Dooley** (Georgia), the national champs and Bowl teams have tended to concoct their own attacking sets. A sample of which system is preferred:

Wishbone: Texas A. & M., Oklahoma, Pennsylvania, Alabama
Veer: Arkansas, UCLA, Pittsburgh, Texas
I-Formation: Ohio State, Michigan, Georgia, Nebraska, USC, Notre Dame, Clemson, Colorado

These systems evolved from a revival in 1940 of the game's oldest formation—the **T**—at Stanford U by Coach **Clark Shaughnessy.** The single and double-wing systems had been the standard collegiate set-up until then. Shaughnessy moved his quarterback up to the center's haunches and placed 3 backs on a line behind the **QB** to form a **T.** He plotted a series of plays in which the **QB** would spin and hand-off quickly to the backs. A man-in-motion halfback opened up a flock of new pass patterns. Speed and quick-openers replaced extended blocking time. When Stanford won every game of its '40 season, the **T** spread nationally.

Plays & Formations

From the straight-T came such innovations as the **Winged-T, Split-T** and the **Wishbone-T.** Of these, the Wishbone is most in vogue today. It was created by **Darrell Royal**, when he coached the University of Texas to the national championship in 1969. Royal moved his fullback up a step from his previous position in the T, giving the backfield the configuration of a wishbone.

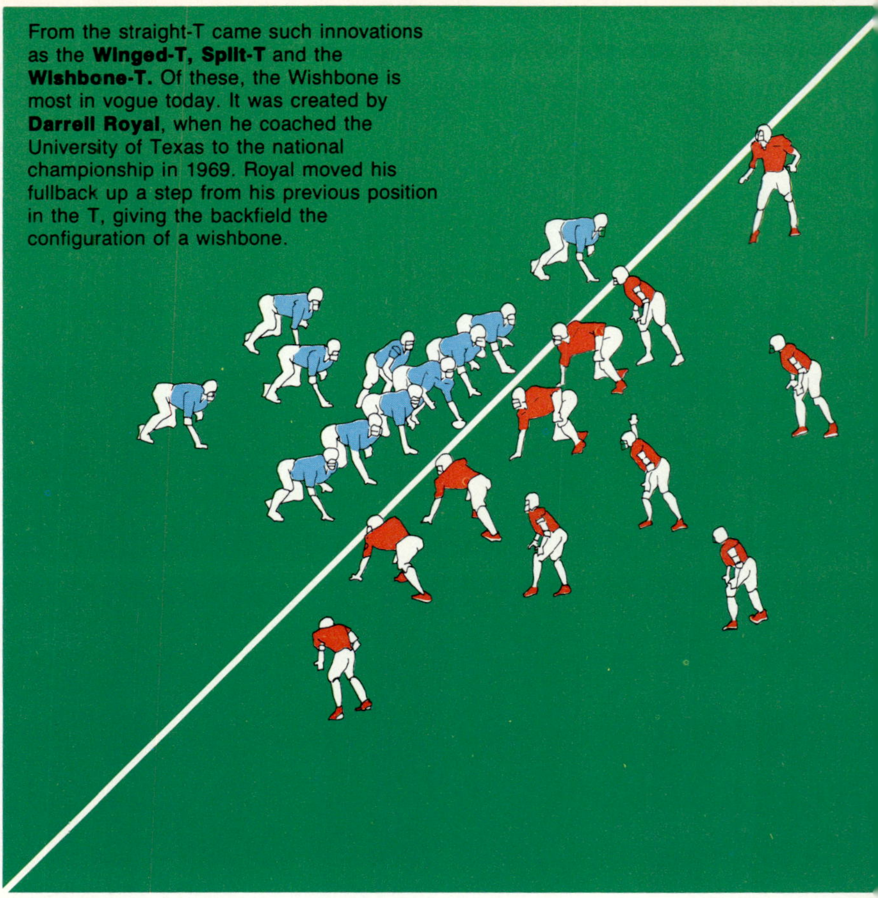

The assorted T-systems look like this:

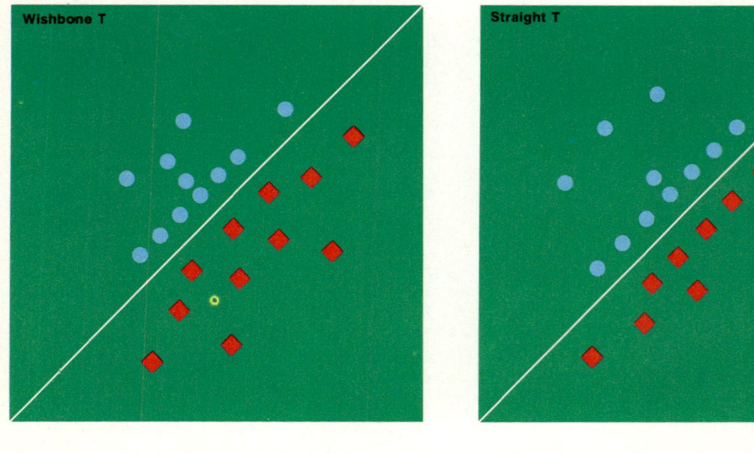

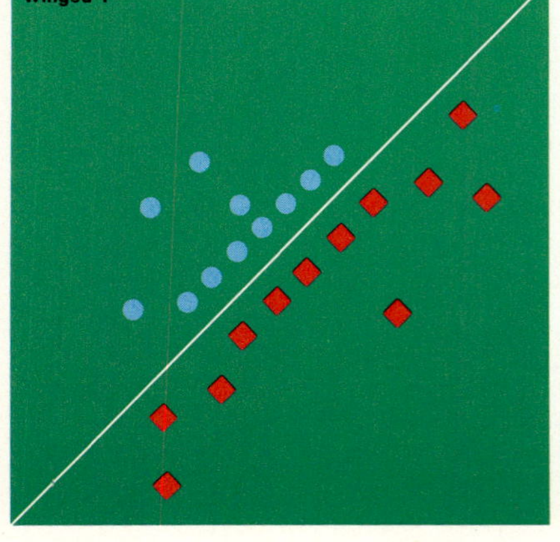

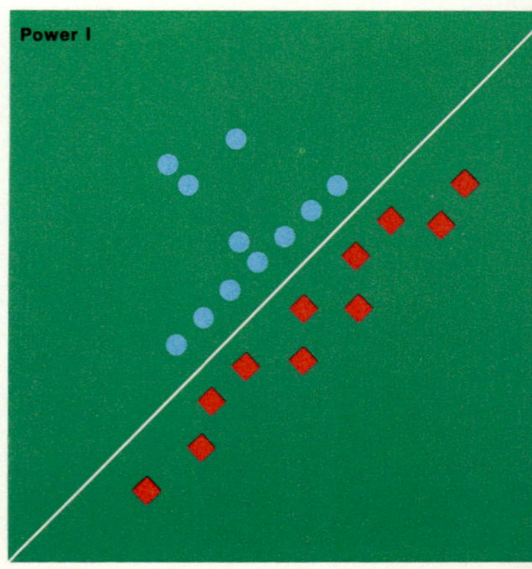

'he pros are scared to death of the option
ılays because they endanger the lives and
'mbs of million-dollar quarterbacks. A
:ollege QB is much more expendable.

-Formation: Johnny McKay, now
:oaching Tampa Bay in the NFL, won 8 and
ost 11 games at USC before he got his **I-**
'ormation installed and working. Using a
'ower-I version, McKay's Trojans won 3
ıational titles and had perfect seasons of
1-0-0 and 12-0-0. The **I** is favored by more
op schools than any other formation. It
eatures an all-purpose tailback and running,
ıassing quarterback, with the former
ıperating behind tandem blockers.

'ro teams rarely use the **quarterback**
ıption or the **triple option.** But colleges
ɔve this daring tactic, which can be run off
he Wishbone or other T-formations. In the
ıuarterback option, the QB is allowed either
o retain the pigskin and advance it

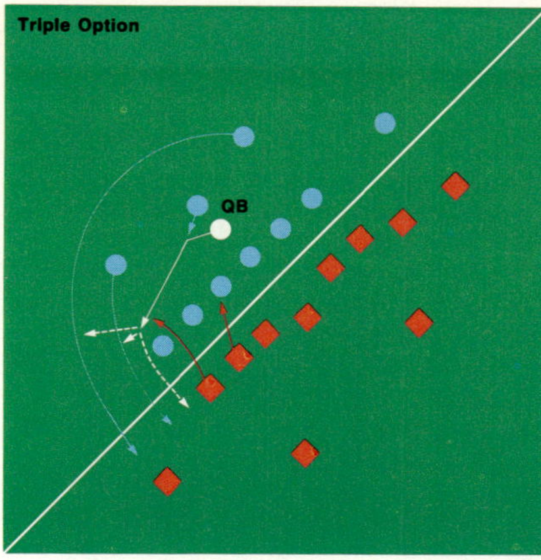

Triple Option

personally, or—if he's well-covered—to pitch it out at the last moment to a back racing laterally behind him. Suspense! Which will he do? In the triple option the QB has 2 ball-carriers he can flip to if he elects not to risk his neck and *tote the mail* himself.

DEFENSE

t isn't true—as some commentators
ırgue—that for every offensive formation
here's a defensive counter, or **alignment.**
On a typical NFL weekend last season,
ome of the scores were 38-13, 24-7, 34-20,
24-0 and 28-10. Clearly, the defenses were
ut to lunch most of the day. The 1981
Super Bowl champion San Francisco 49ers
narched to the crown by such one-sided
allies as 40-17, 41-21, 24-10 and 41-19. Pro
teams have scored as high as 35 points in one quarter, 45 in a half and 72 in a game.

The fact is that defensive coaches have wept tears since 1977, when rule changes robbed them of some of their weapons. Today's 3-4 and 4-3 front alignments by the defense are the latest refinements of long experimentation. The old *Umbrella* and *Diamond* defenses, with 6 and 7 men on the *scrum* (scrimmage line) have been replaced by just a few linemen in the front trenches and 7 or 8 men operating behind them in strategic deployment.

3-4 Defense

Plays & Formations

3-4 defense: At present, 12 NFL teams use the 3-4 as their principal set for foiling the enemy. It calls for only **2 ends** and a **tackle** as front linemen, backed by **4 linebackers**, backed by **4 deep pass-defenders.** It's weak against short passes but effective against long passes, since an extra man is liberated for pass-coverage.

Two of the most-famed alignments are Pittsburgh's *Iron Curtain*, a 4-3, and Denver's *Orange Crush*, a 3-4 setup.

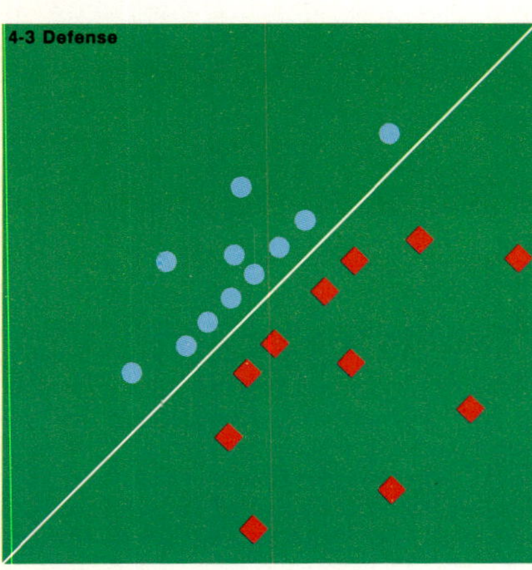

4-3 defense: Here an added man up front puts more pressure on the passer. But it can come up a bit short against the quick look-in or flat pass.

The potent Dallas Cowboys go in for a variation of the **4-3** with their *Doomsday Defense*, in which **3 to 5 linebackers** are used. To form a **flex** alignment, the Cowboys drop their left end back and their right tackle forward to cover the flat passing zone or wide linebacker area.

Safety blitz: There are several types of blitzes in which 2 or more pass-rushers crash in at top speed. The safety blitz is a gamble. It sends a deep **defensive back** in after the QB behind **linemen** who do stunt-blocking to open a passage. But the safety leaves his territory abandoned, wide open for a pass. Additionally, he must reach the scrimmage line just as the ball is snapped—another risky procedure.

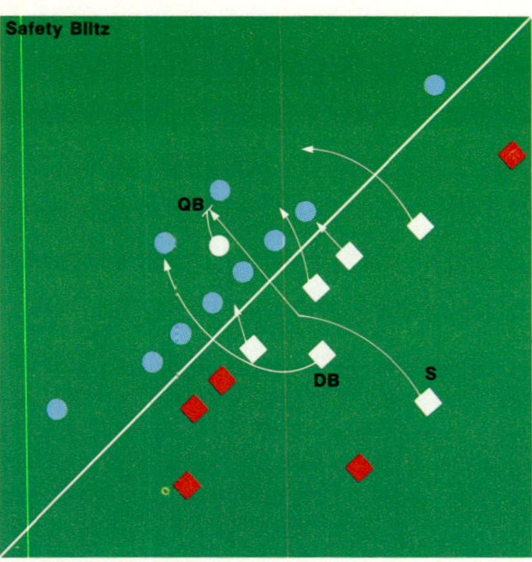

Goal line defense: A compact 6- or 7-man front with linebackers placed in tight to stop the offense when you're pushed back to your goal line. A pass here catches the defense with its pants down. But the odds are that they'll send a fullback type into the line behind **grab-and-shake** blocking (seizing an opponent, shaking him like a dol and forcing an opening). Or, the FB will dive 6 feet high and try to slide the pileup down into the end zone for 6 points.

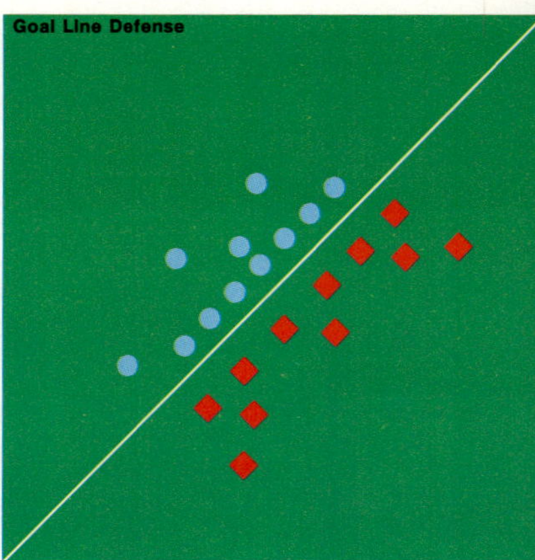

Nickel defense: It's called that because of the injection of a **5th defensive back**, a **roverback** free to go where he sees help is most needed. In a sure-as-hell-it's-a-pass situation, the Nickel gives maximum pass protection.

Prevent defense: TV announcers, for some reason, insist on terming this the PRE-vent maneuver, instead of using the word's proper pronunciation—pre-VENT. Maybe it's because they get excited when teams go into this spread. It comes late in the game when the team on defense is ahead and the attackers are desperate for a scoring pass. So they simply pull back their linebackers, cornermen and safeties to stop the long ball—giving them the short-gain pass and maybe even a first down or 2. But they pre-VENT a touchdown toss. In either a 4-3-2-2 or 3-4-2-2 arrangement:

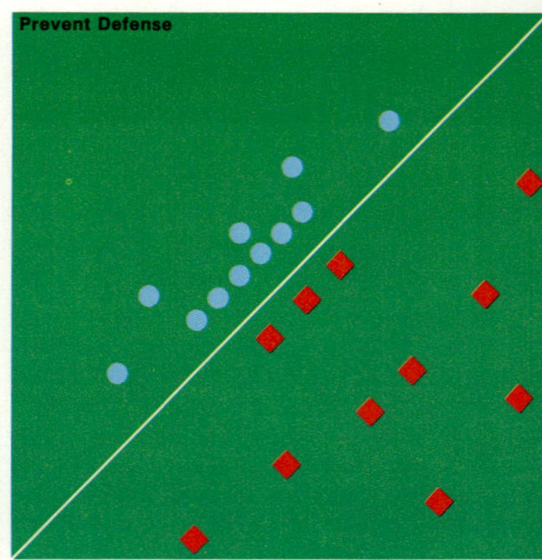

'robabilitles/tendencies: Defensive :aptains, before calling an alignment in the ıuddle to their 10 mates, first consider what **ield zone** they're in. For strategic reasons, he gridiron is split into 3 areas: **high risk, ıormal risk** and **low risk.** The attacking ⅁B usually can be depended upon to call ılays on the basis of which risk sector he's n.

Vithin these 3 sectors there's the **3-down area** and the **4-down area.** In the 3-down, the QB knows that if he doesn't make a first down on 3 plays, he'll be forced to kick on 4th down. But in the 4-down area, he's close enough to the opponent's goal to call a run or pass on 4th down or kick a field goal. In the 3-down region, the offense needs to average 3.33 yards-per-play. In the happy 4-down region, only 2.50 yards-per-play are needed.

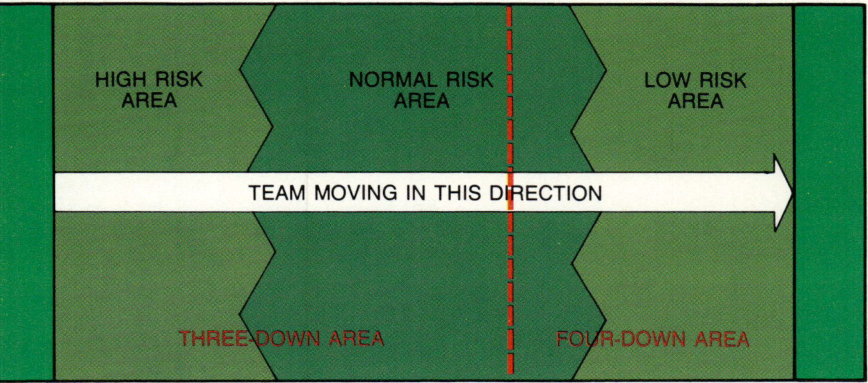

Kicking game: In the average contest of 60-170 plays, the kicking game amounts to ıbout *one-fifth* of all plays: punts, kickoffs, ield goal tries, extra-point conversions, ›nside kicks. Putting the foot into football is :itally important.

'unts: The term comes from English rugby. 'he punt is a semi-defensive measure by he offense. The idea is to boot the ball :afely away, then race down and slaughter he guy catching and returning it. **Time actor:** Pro teams want their center to snap he ball to a kicker standing 15 yards back ı .7 seconds. The punter must get the ball ıirborne in 1.3 seconds. Total: 2 seconds. 'unt coverage sends 8 men downfield. Key nen are the ends, expected to contain the eceiving back inward. If he escapes them, he next widest coverage men are esponsible.

'he punter, himself, takes a wide route lownfield, acting as a *safety* in the event he receiver avoids everybody.

'unters are an odd lot. Some soak their special shoes in water and let them dry on their feet for a *glove* feeling. One kicker, **Tom Dempsey**, had no toes on his kicking foot. Barefoot punters have been known. All of them use the technique of dropping the ball to their ankle-instep at just below waist height...turning the toes inward and downward...and making contact with the foot at just above knee height. The object is **height** more than **distance**, giving the team time to get downfield 40 or 50 yards and corral the receiver. Good *hang time* on a punt is 4.0 to 4.2 seconds.

Kickoff defense: The Kickoff opens the game. This defense can boomerang. In NFL history, more than 30 players have returned kickoffs for 104 or more yards. Dozens more have come back 90 and up. Special kickoff teams are composed of 2 groups of 5 men each, flanking the kicker, and numbered **R-1** to **R-5** and **L-1** to **L-5.** The perimeter men, R-5 and L-5, are assigned to contain the receiving back to the inside, while the other L's and R's are supposed to bury him under 1⅓ tons of flying muscle.

Punting Sequence

Kicker: In 1950, **Pete Gogolak** introduced soccer-style, sideswipe booting at Cornell University and went on to the Buffalo Bills to popularize it. In this technique, the kicker sets up at a 45-degree (or sharper) angle to the ball, takes 2 short, quick steps and on the third step swipe-kicks it into the air. He needs to be an excellent judge of wind and angles.

Most colleges stick with the straight-on *toe kicker.* Overall result: The college record for highest individual average of *career* FGs is 73.2% and for a *season* it's 93%. Comparable NFL figures are lower: 68.6% and 84.4%.

Field goals and conversions: Whether a team uses a sideswiper or straight-on kicker, the 3-point specialists decide many a game. How many? Well, 14 NFC and AFC championship games have been decided by the margin of a couple of field goals. The boys are uncanny. **Jim Bakken** of St. Louis kicked 7 FGs in one game. For Miami, **Garo Yepremium** booted 20 through the crossbars without a miss. **Tony Franklin** of the Philly Eagles split the bars from 59 yards out and **Tom Dempsey** howitzered one 63 yards for New Orleans (the NFL distance record).

On the collegiate front, **Ish Ordonez** of Arkansas kicked 16 in a row and **Charley Gogolak** of Princeton registered 6 FGs in an afternoon of work. **Russ Erxleben** of Texas set the distance mark of 67 yards (tied by 2 others).

Some fans despise FGs as a rotten way to settle a violent game. Only three men are involved in a field goal attempt—the ball-snapper, holder and kicker—and, to top it off, football has been invaded by bandy-legged, 150-pounders who come from the European soccer field and kick with their insteps instead of their toes! "These shrimps sit on the bench all day," said Detroit lineman Alex Karras, "and then say 'I theenk I go keek a touchdown.' They don't even know the goddam rules." Hailing from such spots as Hungary, Cyprus, East Germany and Norway, these imports have revolutionized 3-point style.

TV viewers and *live* fans should pay close attention to one factor: *the snap of the ball.* That's the secret of the successful placekick from the field, from 25 yards to 60. The **holder**, usually a **quarterback** or **defensive back** with *good* (sure) hands, crouches on one knee from 6½ to 7 yds back of center. The ball should come in low, at knee height. If the holder must reach up, pull down the ball and set it up, the FG ma[y] well be blocked. **1.3** seconds is the averag[e] total time allowed for the entire operation, from snap to hold to kick.

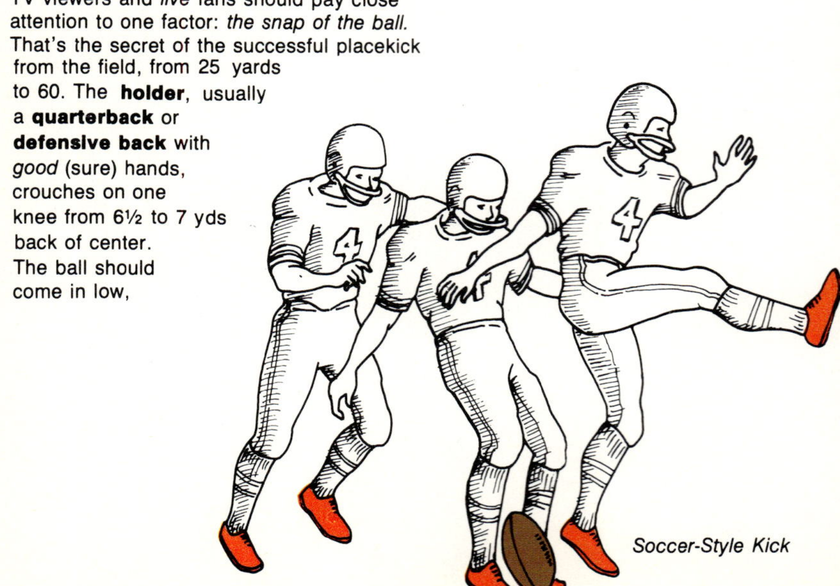

Soccer-Style Kick

Blocking on FGs: At the snap, the **tight ends, tackles, guards** and **center** charge forward. Their job is to lay on a sound hit t[o] keep the defense out of balance and away from flight of the ball while it's gaining altitude. **Close-up backs** must fend off the outside rush.

Attackers: They're coming in like gangbusters. The idea is for 2 outside men, an **end** and **tackle**, to be given a shot at blocking the ball through action of adjacent linemen.

Holder: He is required—or the kicker will scream at him in a foreign language—to se[t] the ball straight up with the laces *away* fro[m] the kicker. A smooth kicking surface is wanted. The holder uses just his index finger with light but firm pressure to positio[n] the ball. He quickly rotates a spinning ball into a laces-away mode. On long kicks of 4[0] or more yards, if the laces are on one side and not forward, the ball will curve to the lace side—often causing a miss.

Foreign Invasion

There was a time, not long ago, when the pros hailed almost 100 per cent from one o[f] the 50 American states. Now they spring from such farflung global points that it seems NATO, OAS and the UN are doing the scouting.

Recent NFL rosters have included players from:

Bologna, **Italy**
Okinawa, **Japan**
Fetsund, **Norway**
Lamaca, **Cyprus**
Havana, **Cuba**
Pago Pago, **Samoa**
Guatemala City, **Guat.**
Halifax, **Nova Scotia**
Asuncion, **Paraguay**
Munich, **Germany**
Istanbul, **Turkey**
Wexford, **Ireland**
Vienna, **Austria**
Bellshill, **Scotland**
Mexico City, **Mexic[o]**
Belgrade, **Yugoslav[ia]**
Bogota, **Colombia**
Leeds, **England**
Tapei, **Taiwan**
Cardiff, **Wales**

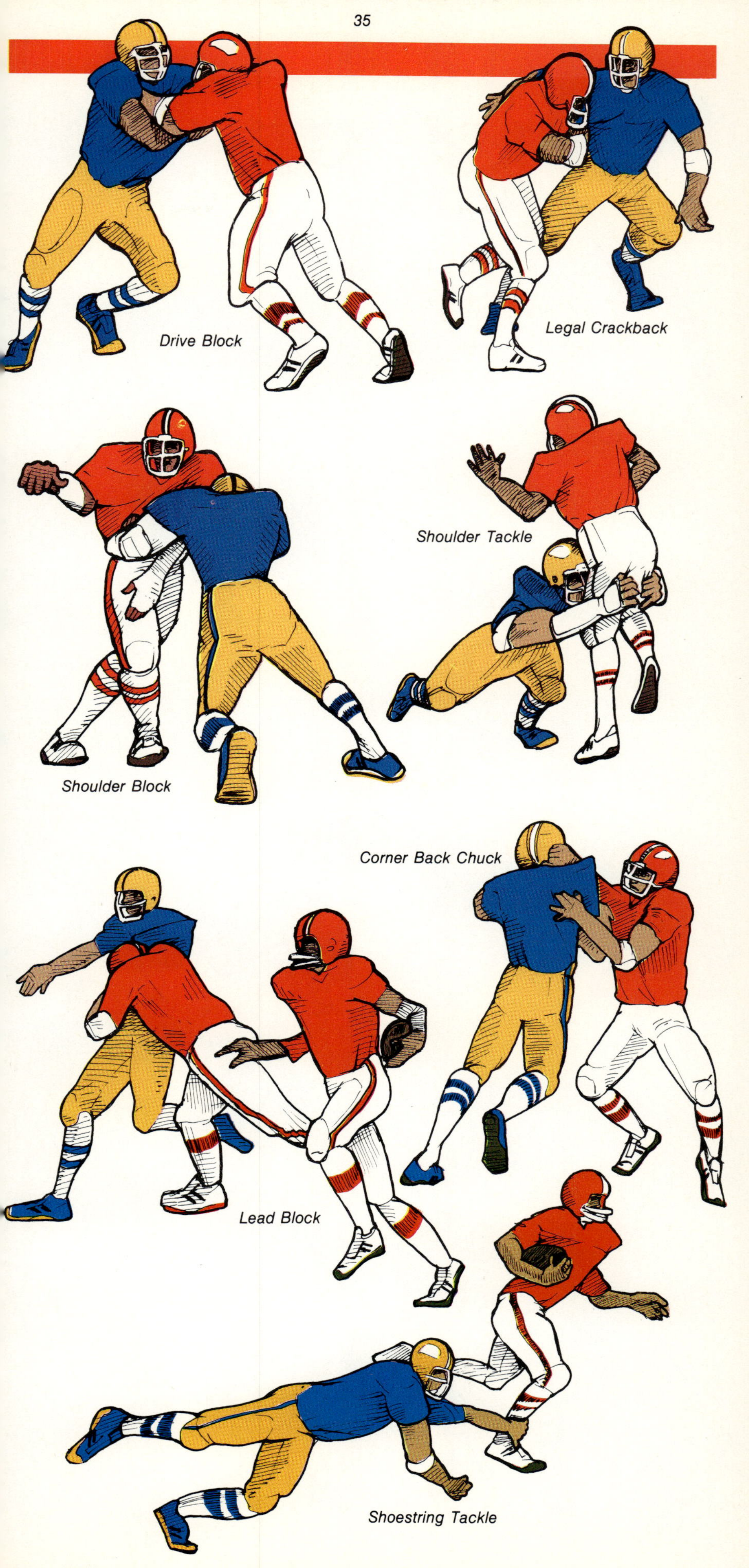
Drive Block
Legal Crackback
Shoulder Tackle
Shoulder Block
Corner Back Chuck
Lead Block
Shoestring Tackle

Hook Block
Suicide or
Scramble Block
Double Team
Straight Arm
Submarine Block
Gang Tackle

Stripping the Ball Arm Lock

Cross Tackle

Fumble

Plugging the Gap

Sack

Most Americans had yet to see a television set when pro football's first *tube* game premiered in New York City.

It was October 22, 1939, a cloudy day in Manhattan. An NBC affiliate, W2XBS, telecast the Philadelphia Eagles vs. the Brooklyn Dodgers live from Ebbets Field.

The foggy picture created a sensation. So new was TV that fewer than 1,000 New Yorkers owned sets. Many of the players on the field were unaware they were on camera. At times during the game, screens went blank and W2XBS was forced to revert to a radio broadcast.

"But it was such a terrific battle," recalled **Allen Waltz**, who did the play-by-play, "that those who saw it wanted more." The Dodgers beat the Eagles, 23-14, with 5 famous players taking part: **Ace Parker, Pug Manders, Perry Schwartz, Bill Hewitt** and **Davey O'Brien.**

From that modest start, TV and football became partners—an industry soon to be measured in megamillions of dollars. Historical highlights:

1960: ABC and the NFL signed a 5-year contract for telecasting several selected games.

1962: The NFL and CBS signed for telecasting all regular-season games for $4.65 million annually.

1964: CBS entered the winning bid of $14.1 million per year for regular-season rights for 2 years.

1966: Rights to the Super Bowl telecast were sold to NBC and CBS for 4 years for $9.5 million.

1969: Monday night telecasts were set for 1970-71-72, with rights to 13 games acquired by ABC.

1971: The Super Bowl VI telecast drew 23,980,000 viewers, the largest audience to see a single sports event.

1973: Super Bowl VII pulled a 75,000,000 audience, a dramatic increase from the past 2 years. Partially because of a growing TV audience, the NFL introduced a numbering system for players. Quarterbacks and kickers were numbered 1-19; running and defensive backs, 20-49; centers and linebackers, 50-59; defensive linemen and interior offensive linemen, 60-79; wide receivers and tight ends, 80-89.

1974: A blow to the NFL—Congress ruled as experimental legislation that any game to which tickets were available 120 hours prior to kickoff and that had been sold out 72 hours prior to kickoff must be made available for local telecast.

1975: The NFL sold 10,236,322 tickets for 182 regular-season games, a slight decline from 1974. Of that total, 1,124,162 tickets, or 11 per cent, were not used by *no-show* fans. The lure of watching games on TV was blamed.

1976: The Super Bowl viewing audience reached 80 million—the largest audience for any TV show of any type.

1977: In the largest single TV package ever negotiated, NBC, CBS and ABC divided rights for 4 years to regular, postseason, Pro Bowl and Super Bowl games for a reported $640 million.

1981: Each NFL team received $5.6 million in TV revenue and the forecast was made that league income would escalate to nearly $2 billion after 1982. This prediction was more than borne out (see *Salaries*).

The techniques: Comfortably ensconced in a home easy chair, viewers are treated to a marvel of the electronics science—detailed camerawork which misses very little. TV'd football came of age in this manner:

1960: ABC pioneered the light, **hand-held camera.** With a newfangled *creepie-peepie* lens-pack on his back, **Mike Freedman** of ABC strolled the sidelines at a Duke-UCLA game. For the first time, closeups of sweaty, banged-up players and snarling coaches were brought into living rooms. "They even photograph my dental fillings!" beefed UCLA Coach **Bill Barnes**.

1963: Video tape had just been introduced to TV. CBS director **Tony Verna** had an idea: to stay with the quarterbacks on every play with one camera for possible later showing. Luckily, Army's QB **Rollie Stichweh** scored a touchdown on Navy, himself. Verna at once showed it to viewers—and the **isolated playback** was born.

1964: All networks began to place cameras in end zones to further isolate pass-receivers, defenders, linebackers. etc., bringing on full **instant replay.** Stop-action, or **freeze-frame**, followed.

1975: By now, ABC had gone from 6 cameras to 10, broadly expanding upon the primary-action lens stationed on the 50-yard line. **Behind-goalpost perspective** was a popular twist.

1978: TV got down on its belly with **field-level** camera angles, bringing viewers onto the field and into the thick of the combat. Great on kickoffs.

1980s: A host of new techniques emerged. ***High-aerials*** from the Goodyear blimps were upstaged. In 1981 at Super Bowl XV, NBC Sports brought forth its **Louma**. This exotic gadget consists of a tall crane with a swivel camera fixed to a prehensile arm. Prohibited from crossing the dotted yellow lines around team benches, NBC could extend the Louma outward by remote control to peek down on players' and coaches' tortured expressions. Sensational!

At Super Bowl XVI came CBS's **Renfro 82.** This camera gives a double look at disputed plays, such as a TD pass caught either inside or outside of the end zone. (It's named for **Mike Renfro** of the Houston Oilers, who in 1980 figured in a disputed end zone catch.) The Renfro gives a **reverse-angle replay**—a view of a very tough play to call—from the opposite side of the initial picture.

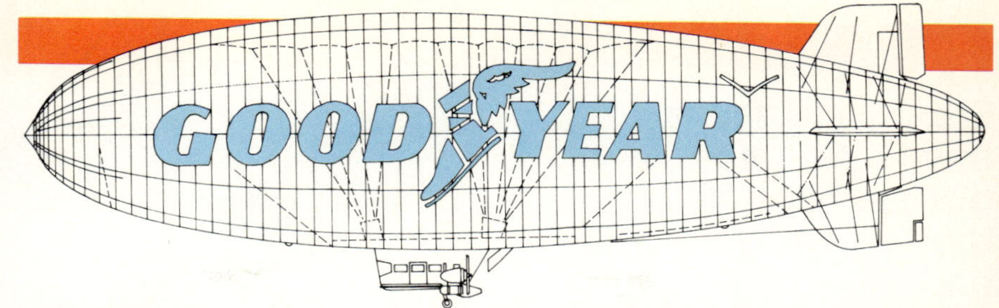

The **Telestrator** is a chalkboard used by ex-NFL coach (and now CBS commentator) **John Madden** to quickly diagram and explain plays as they happen. Rather technical—but interesting to many. Also, after complaints of too much gabbing by announcing teams, TV has come to the **silent telecast.** NBC experimented with no talking at all, just the pictures, in a 1981 Miami-New York Jets clash. Most home fans didn't like the *eerie silence.* Neither did **Howard Cosell.**

What will electronic engineers hit on next? Cameras sunk into the field which pop up like periscopes for *flash* shots? A metal chip placed in footballs to light up a *T* on your screen when the ball penetrates the goal line—ending all argument? Both these ideas are under study for *The Eye's* future.

America's Favorite Pastime—Bowlwatching!

One third of TV's all-time audience draws have been Super Bowls, leaving no doubt that in the U.S., football is **The Game.**

Alltime Rating	Superbowl	Percentage of Households Watching	Network
3	XVI	49.1	CBS
6	XII	47.2	CBS
7	XIII	47.1	NBC
9	XIV	46.3	CBS
16(tie)	XI/XV	44.4/44.3	NBC
18	VI	44.2	CBS
26	VII	41.7	CBS
27	IX	42.4	CBS
29	X	42.3	CBS

(Superbowl XII Pregame Show rated 42.1)

Football's Million Dollar Minute.

Traditionally each Super Bowl game sets a new record in the cost of TV advertising, and 1981 was no exception. During Super Bowl XVI, 30 seconds of nationwide network advertising cost $345,000. 1982 Super Bowl sponsors will pay an estimated **$1,000,000 per minute** to bring their products to America's attention.

1982: ABC and ESPN gave credibility to the new U.S. Football League with their purchase of the telecasting rights for combined airing of 3 games weekly beginning March, 1983.

Growth: When video science was young, 2 or 3 CBS, ABC and NBC cameras were deemed sufficient to cover game action. What changes time has wrought! At the 1982 Super Bowl bash, CBS employed 16 cameras of every variety, located from the upper reaches to the floor of Detroit's Silverdome. More than $10 million worth of production equipment was manned by more than 80 technicians. Fourteen replay machines were needed. CBS's budget for Super Bowl XVI reportedly was $2 million.

The Tube's Bonanza: CBS paid $6 million to the NFL for telecast rights to *Super* XVI. Thirty-seven minutes of advertising was aired. Fees ranged from $130,000 for a 30-second message (pre-game show) to $345,000 for a 30-second spot (gametime), according to industry sources. All records were smashed. The $345,000 pricetag for half-minute ad slots far surpassed the $285,000 fee at the 1981 Super Bowl. Some 45 per cent of America's 81 million TV households tuned in—an audience of well over 100 million.

The NFL's Position: In 1978, Commissioner **Pete Rozelle** negotiated telecast rights to all league games for an overall network price of $640 million. Upon that contract's expiration in '82, the price leaped to a reported $2 billion for 5 years. Income to each of 28 teams in the league will average from $14 to $15 million per season. (Or roughly one-fourth the value of a top, modern NFL franchise.)

The NCAA's Position: For 1982 the colleges go to a 2-network format (ABC now joined by CBS). The nets will pay a combined $132 million rights fee per season, from 1982-1985, a 110 per cent increase over previous charges. A nationally televised game will now be worth $1 million to $1.2 million to each school, a regional telecast upward of $700,000. Among bowls, the Rose Bowl commands the No.1 payoff—$5.2 million from NBC for the 1983 event. The Cotton Bowl's $3.5 million ranks second.

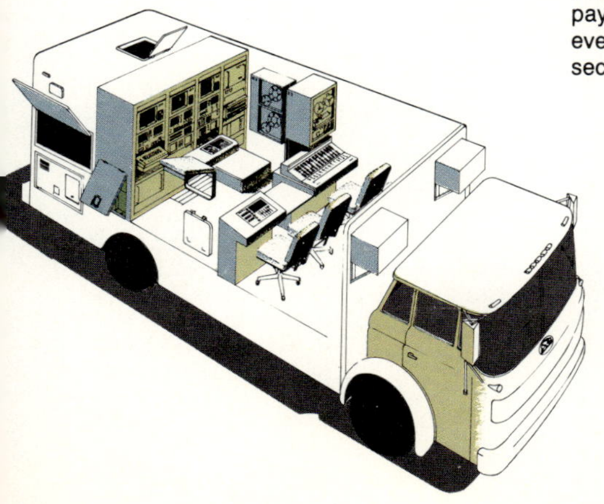

In 1950 the LA Rams signed an agreement with Admiral TV that permitted televising of their games. One stipulation of the agreement was that any loss of revenue caused by fans staying at home to watch on TV would be made up by the sponsoring advertiser. (TV's impact was determined by comparison of box office receipts with those from the year before.) Admiral ended up paying approximately $300,000.

Stadia

From ramshackle municipal parks and dirt semipro lots to the largest enclosed and air-warmed stadium on earth—that's the NFL story in less than half a century. Arena-building boomed across the U.S. because of football's draw.

In 1925, **Red Grange** and the Chicago Bears pulled 70,000 vs. the New York Giants at the Polo Grounds, N.Y. That was the game's first huge audience. It opened eyes to a tremendous potential.

But stadium bond money was hard to find. In 1934, the NFL attracted only 512,000 fans for a per-game average of 8,211. Today—with pigskin palaces rising everywhere—attendance has passed 16.5 million and averages more than to 60,000 per game.

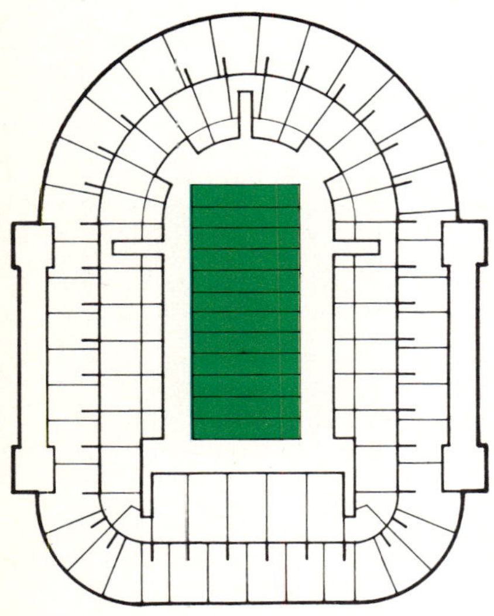

Oldest NFL stadium
Soldier Field (Chicago Bears), opened 1926.

The ***great domes***, bringing the game indoors, free of rain and snow and under climate-control, are the most dramatic trend in stadia:

Louisiana Superdome (New Orleans Saints, opened 1975): Dwarfing the Astrodome, it covers 13 acres, with 9 tons of computerized air-conditioning equipment and towering so high that a 25-story building could fit under its vast arch. Capacity: 80,400—71,330 for football. The largest unobstructed room ever built by man at the time, the Superdome introduced instant replay screens. *The cost—$2,224 per seat ($121.6 million total)*—brought screams and lawsuits from taxpayers. But *Superbarn* sells out regularly.

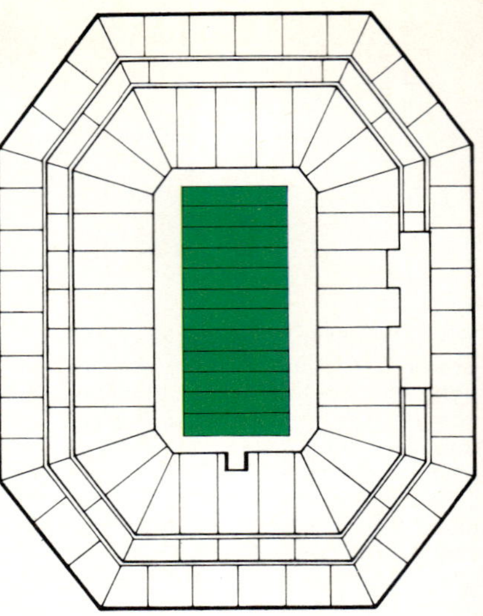

Silverdome (Detroit Lions, opened 1976): The largest domed structure on earth, it holds 80,638. Located in Pontiac, Michigan, 20 miles north of Detroit, its *Saran Wrap* roof rises 205 feet above the field—a fabric dome supported by pumped air, not by steel. *This helped hold cost to $529 per seat ($55.7 million.)* A 1976 tornado deflated the roof, which fell 105 feet during a game. The game went on, anyway.

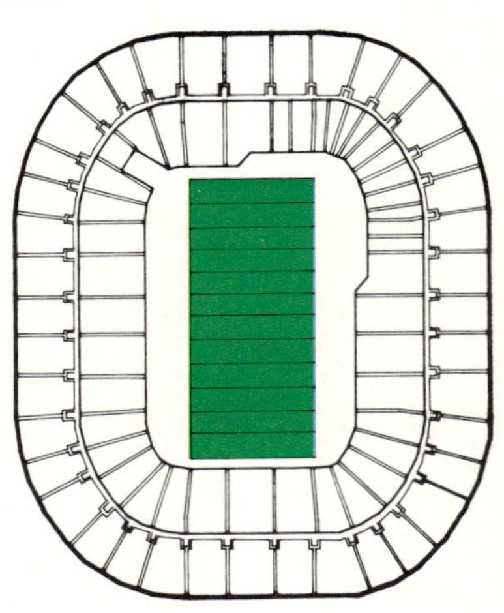

Minneapolis Metrodome (Minnesota Vikings, opened 1982): Latest of the domes, this $55 million arena was built to keep the Vikings from moving to a less-chilly climate. Football capacity: 62,212. Formerly named the **Hubert H. Humphrey Metrodome**, it rises 16 stories and at the lowest level is 47 feet below outside streets. Like the other domes, it has luxury boxes for special clients—115 of them.

Arrowhead Stadium (Kansas City Chiefs, opened 1972): Part of a twin-arena sports complex costing $75 million when opened, Arrowhead is a magnificent 78,000-seater and has won numerous architectural prizes. Kansas City Chiefs' owner, oilman **Lamar Hunt**, helped finance Arrowhead. The story goes that his father, billionaire **H.L. Hunt**, was told that Lamar was losing $1 million per year on football. Replied **H.L. Hunt,** "Well, at that rate he can't last longer than 150 years."

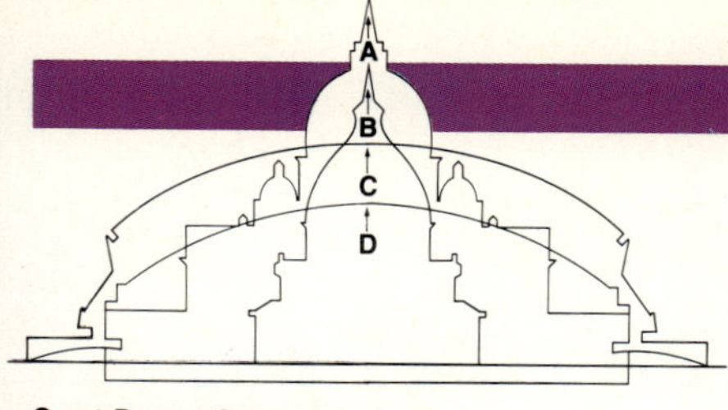

Great Domes Compared:
A—Saint Peter's Basilica, Italy
B—Duomo in Florence, Italy
C—Silverdome
D—Astrodome

Houston Astrodome (Houston Oilers, opened 1965): With a winning club in the Oilers, citizens built the *Taj Mahal* of stadia. *Cost: $38 million.* While limited to 50,452 capacity, the Astrodome was the first roofed arena, had a 72-degree fixed temperature and was an instant hit.

High-capacity NFL stadia

Largest in the NFL are **Detroit's Silverdome, Cleveland Stadium, Buffalo's Rich Stadium** and **Kansas City's Arrowhead Stadium.** For college play, the Michigan U stadium and the **Los Angeles Coliseum** can handle upward of 90,000 fans. Smallest is the Minnesota Vikings' Metro Stadium at 48,446.

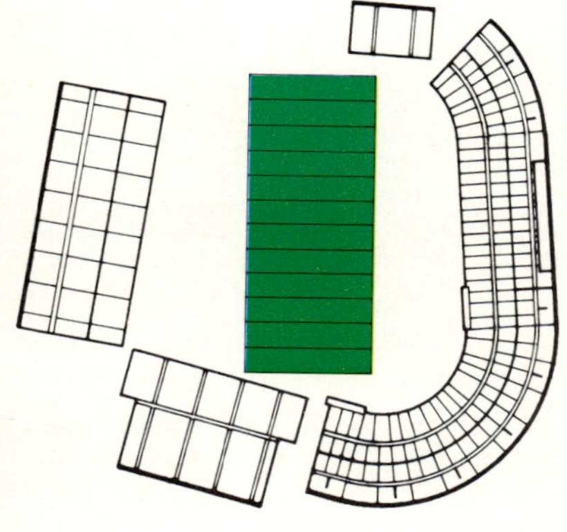

Playing surfaces

Although in a poll 84 per cent of NFL players said they preferred natural grass to artificial surfaces, the synthetic field is here to stay. Fake turf was first introduced at the Astrodome, Houston, in 1966.

The complaint is that, because of their hardness, synthetic fields cause *hot feet,* burns to hands, and bone and tendon injuries. In 1970, the NFL Players Association took the matter to the National Labor Relations Board as a grievance. In the end, the players lost. The current breakdown on fields:

1. Teams with **AstroTurf:** 10
2. Teams with **Tartan Turf:** 2
3. Teams with **Super Turf** or **Texas Turf:** 2
4. Teams with **grass:** 14

(an equal division: 14 synthetic, 14 grass)

Strangest Incident

Franklin Field at the University of Pennsylvania, Philadelphia: In 1969, when the Philadelphia Eagles met the Washington Redskins on a newly-laid synthetic field, thousands of dead grasshoppers had to be hosed away before play could start. The grasshoppers thought the green stuff was good to eat and starved to death.

Stadia Attendance: After yielding some ground to pro football in the mid-1970s, Division 1-A members of the NCAA have made a strong comeback. In 1975, the colleges drew 31.6 million fans. That shot up to more than 36 million in 1981. While many campuses felt a money squeeze when all-sport budgets reached 4 million dollars annually, and some dropped football, 642 schools still fielded grid teams in the 1980s.

In 1981 NFL attendance finally topped 60,000 average-per-game, beating the 59,787 record set in 1980.

Average Top-10 per-game attendance at College Stadia, 1980-1981

1. **Michigan: 104,292**
2. **Tennessee: 88,649**
3. **Ohio State: 87,925**
4. **Penn State: 83,045**
5. **Nebraska: 76,047**
6. **Oklahoma: 74,449**
7. **Louisiana State: 74,117**
8. **Wisconsin: 71,361**
9. **Alabama: 70,888**
10. **Michigan State: 70,092**

The largest crowd to watch a collegiate game since records were kept: Michigan vs. Ohio State, 1979: 106,255 (regular season).

Highest total home attendance: Michigan, 1979: 730,315

Most consecutive home sellout crowds: Nebraska, 112

Other major modern constructions

Buffalo Bills: In 1973 the Bills erected one of the largest outdoor facilities—**Rich Stadium**, with an 80,020 capacity.

Seattle Seahawks: Roofed, central-city **Kingdome** seats 64,757, and since 1977, has been sold out game after game. Its the only West Coast domed arena for football.

Tampa Bay: Granted an expansion franchise in 1976, the Buccaneers are housed in spacious **Tampa Stadium**, a scenic, sheer-comfort stadium with 72,128 theater-type seats.

Pro Football Stadia Capacities:

Detroit	**Pontiac Silverdome**	**80,638**
Cleveland	Cleveland Stadium	80,322
Buffalo	Rich Stadium	80,020
Kansas City	Arrowhead Stadium	78,067
N.Y. Giants	Giants Stadium	76,891
Miami	Orange Bowl	75,459
Denver	Mile-High Stadium	75,103
Tampa Bay	Tampa Stadium	72,128
Philadelphia	Philadelphia Veterans Stadium	71,524
New Orleans	Louisiana Superdome	71,330
Los Angeles	Anaheim Stadium	69,005
Dallas	Texas Stadium	65,101
Seattle	Kingdome	64,757
Chicago	Soldier Field	64,519
Minnesota	Minneapolis Metrodome	62,212
New England	Schaefer Stadium	61,297
San Francisco	Candlestick Park	61,185
Atlanta	Atlanta-Fulton County Stadium	60,748
Baltimore	Memorial Stadium	60,714
N.Y. Jets	Shea Stadium	60,372
Cincinnati	Riverfront Stadium	59,754
Green Bay	Lambeau Field	56,191
Green Bay	Milwaukee County Stadium	55,958
Washington	Robert F. Kennedy Stadium	55,045
Oakland	Oakland-Alameda Coliseum	54,616
Pittsburgh	Three Rivers Stadium	54,000
San Diego	Jack Murphy Stadium	52,675
St. Louis	Busch Memorial Stadium	51,392
Houston	Astrodome	50,452

Salaries

Pick-ax-wielding coalminers did better than hired gridmen in the 1920s and 30s.

"I got $125 per game in 1931," reported **Mel Hein**, who became a Hall of Fame center with the New York Giants. That was for 14 games, or $1,750 for the season.

Only a few flamboyant heroes of 50-60 years ago had big-money contracts. **Red Grange**, an American idol, made $12,000 in one game (per cent of the box office) and $50,000 for a movie on his life.

1940s: Salaries hadn't improved much. But there were exceptions. ***Bullet* Bill Dudley** of Virginia drew $20,000 per season from the Detroit Lions, said to be the richest of NFL contracts. Today, $20,000 wouldn't pay the adhesive tape bill ($35,000) for one pro squad per season.

1950s: One of the legendary fullbacks, **Marlon Motley**, averaged 5 yards-per-carry, earned $11,500 per season at his peak. Other stars, who'd never see $15,000 in their careers, spoke of forming a union.

1960: Competition for college headliners grew. Heisman Trophy winner **Billy Cannon** of Louisiana State accepted $100,000 from the Houston Oilers over hot bidding by many teams.

1962: The NFLPA (Players Association) was formed and fought for a minimum leaguewide salary of $13,000 and $300-per-week training-camp expenses. By 1968, the NFLPA achieved this goal.

1965: New York Jets owner **Sonny Werblin** shocked the world by creating the *package*—bonus for signing, a fancy car, salary, other perks—and inked **Joe Namath** out of Alabama U for $427,000. Werblin paid $200,000 to a second quarterback, **John Huarte** of Notre Dame. It was the breakthrough players had long awaited.

1969: Werblin's generosity didn't brush off in a big way. In the wake of the NFL-AFL rivalry and war for talent, the average league salary stood at $22,000. But the art of holding out for more dollars or signing with the Canadian Football League produced such results as fullback **Larry Csonka's** $110,000, 3-year pact with the Miami Dolphins and defenseman **Johnny Sample's** $120,000 for 3 years with Baltimore. At draft time players hired lawyer-agents to negotiate for them—a wise, if controversial, move.

1972: The median pro paycheck moved up—but not much—from the $22,000 of 1969 to $30,100. Many rookies and reserves played for half of that.

1976: O.J. Simpson, the *perfect running back* and hottest item in cleats, was drafted out of USC by a team he didn't want, the Buffalo Bills. Simpson stayed with Buffalo long enough to collect a reported **$806,000** per season. The era of *superdough* had arrived.

Bob Nash, Akron Lineman, was the first player to be *dealt* when he was sent to Buffalo for $300.00 and 5% of gate receipts.

The first NFL franchises cost **$100.00 each.**

1980s: Simpson's take is still alleged to be the highest compensation ever paid out for a single season of play. According to the National Football League's Management Council, as of early 1982 the most highly rewarded athletes on a per season basis are:

1. **Archie Manning,** *QB, New Orleans,* **$600,000**
2. **Walter Payton,** *RB, Chicago,* **$500,000**
3. **Ken Stabler,** *QB, Houston,* **$470,000**
4. ***Bob Griese,** *QB, Miami,* **$415,025**
5. **Ron Jaworski,** *QB, Philadelphia,* **$410,000**
6. **Joe Ferguson,** *QB, Buffalo,* **$396,000**
7. **George Rogers,** *RB, New Orleans,* **$375,000**
8. **Billy Sims,** *RB, Detroit,* **$352,500**
9. **Franco Harris,** *RB, Pittsburgh,* **$350,000**
10. **Lynn Swann,** *WR, Pittsburgh,* **$340,000**

*Retired, but contract guaranteed.

Note: Many of the highest-ranked performers of 1982 do not appear on this list. They do not yet have the years of service behind them that most of the above players do. Time-in-service counts heavily in salary stipulations.

While a minor percentage of NFLPA members are drawing $300,000 or more per campaign, the current *average* is another story. In 1982, says the NFL Management Council, average pay for approximately 1,260 active players at all positions is $90,102, up 14.5 per cent from $78,657, in 1981.

Charted here are 1972 and 1982 average salaries by position:

Position	1972 average	1982 average
Quarterbacks	$41,500	**$160,037**
Running backs	33,500	**94,948**
Offensive linemen	26,600	**85,543**
Defensive linemen	26,900	**92,961**
Receivers	29,100	**85,873**
Linebackers	26,700	**85,205**
Defensive backs	25,500	**79,581**
Kickers	22,800	**65,779**

Biggest gains over the past 10 years were made by men at positions hardest to fill: quarterback, defensive lineman and defensive back. The QBs with an $118,537 average increase benefited the most.

The highest-paid individuals, other than the quarterbacks and running backs shown on the above *Top 10* list, are, in 1982:

Defensive lineman: **Randy White**, Dallas, $318,750
Offensive lineman: **Claudie Minor**, Denver, $226,250
Linebacker: **Jack Ham**, Pittsburgh, $299,667
Kicker: **Mark Moseley**, Washington, $143,000

Battle for more money: The NFLPA Executive Director **Ed Garvey** points out that while the NFL pay average is between $82,000 and $100,000, in pro basketball the figure is $190,000; in pro baseball, $143,000; and in pro hockey, $108,000. Players feel it is unfair that they are paid *so little* comparatively. Arguments include the fact that 93 per cent of NFL seats were sold in 1981 and that the NFL's most recent television contract, worth $2 billion over the next 5 years, brings $14 million to $15 million to each team per year. Individual team payrolls of from $3.5 million to $4.2 million are insufficient, claims the NFLPA.

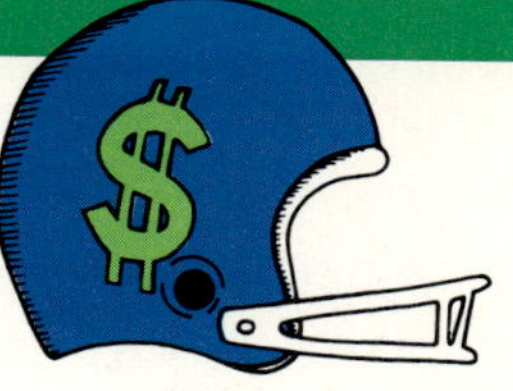

Management retorts that you can't compare football with the other sports. Each club pays 55 men per season (including the reserve *taxi squad*) compared to 25 for baseball and a dozen for basketball. And the NFL gets income from 16 regular season games compared to 162 for baseball and 82 for basketball. Other factors enter in, making for a stormy NFL-NFLPA conflict at the present time.

Where does the loot go? After paying their agents varying-sized commissions, the highest-earning pros often become one-man conglomerates, investing in stocks, real estate, auto agencies, restaurants and the like. Income reaching $500,000 annually for product endorsements is not uncommon among the big-name performers. The NFLPA reports that its members are also involved in wineries, sportscasting, cattle ranching, tungsten mining, oil and gas wells, import-export, aircraft and car-leasing, food franchising and movie deals. No figures are available on how many millionaires exist among active and recently retired pros—but one guess is that they exceed 100.

Coaches: As a group, coaches are coy about revealing their incomes. Colleges and pro-team owners try to protect this information. However, it's believed that NFL salaries run between $200,000 and $400,000 per season for the head man and up to a $1.4 million payroll for an entire staff of 10-11 assistants and the boss.

Possibly the highest base salary in major college football is the $105,000 said to be paid to Alabama's ***Bear Bryant***, whose total income (including fees from media sources and miscellaneous perquisites) is close to $450,000.

On the average, $50,000-$60,000 is earned by collegiate grid coaches, plus they reap much more with their own TV and radio shows, summer camps and lucrative investments arranged by the alumni.

One southern coach sued for a $400,000 claimed loss in fringe benefits when he was fired. Forever on the spot, campus grid profs last only an average of 6.5 seasons on the job. The trend toward jumping to the pro league grows: **Don Coryell** (San Diego), **Johnny McKay** (Tampa Bay), **Dick Vermeil** (Philadelphia) and **Bill Walsh** (San Francisco) are among those who abandoned the collegiate ranks.

Scouting: Considering the financial outlay that teams make for players' salaries, it is not unusual that statistics, computer programs, economics, politics, geography, intuition and just plain luck all contribute in varying degrees to scouting decisions in the search for new talent.

A sample questionnaire that a pro scout might use:

OFFENSIVE BACK

Name ______________________________

School ______________________________

Height __________ Weight __________ Age __________

Time __________ Distance __________ Gear __________

Did Player run with someone? ______________________________

	Fits him to a "T"	A lot like him	Moderately like him	A bit like him	Doesn't fit him at all
He doesn't always cooperate					
He is quick as a cat					
He wants to win at all costs					
He finally catches on after much repetition					
He is strong as a bull					
He rarely thinks of anyone but himself					
He will break his neck to carry out assignments					
He can retain what he has learned					
He can overpower a man of equal strength by brute force					
He would just as soon miss practice					
He digs in and you can't move him					

Prospects of Playing Pro Football:

cinch
real good
good
slim
none

Coaches — Professional Football

The name of George Halas stands before all other coaches for durability. Only 15 coaches in pro history have won more than 100 games. And Halas, who coached the Chicago Bears for 40 seasons and currently is the club's board chairman, is far in front with 326 victories.

George Halas: Grandpappy of the game, his Chicago Bears took 7 NFL titles; the only person to be associated with the league from its 1920 inception to the present day. Co-invented the T-Formation and man-in-motion. His *Monsters of the Midway* in the early 1940s powered to 37 wins in 42 starts.

Earl *Curly* Lambeau: Also a pioneer, he coached the Green Bay Packers for 31 years. Lambeau was an offensive specialist who made the foward pass a deadly weapon. He was first to win 3 straight NFL crowns (1929-30-31).

Chuck Noll: The NFL's quiet man, Noll is near the top in modern football statistics with 131 Pittsburgh Steeler game wins in 13 campaigns. He teaches power football with emphasis on fullback charges behind intricate blocking and flashy pass patterns. Noll is king of the Super Bowl with 4 diamond rings on his fingers, no defeats and repeat victories (1975-76, 1979-80).

Tom Landry: A B-17 bomber pilot in World War II, he both *bombs* opponents with the long ball and features the much-copied *flex* defense (odd spacing of 7 down linemen) with the Dallas Cowboys. Wearing *lucky* hats, Landry is an exponent of the *Shotgun* offense. He has 13 Division championships or co-titles and 2 Super Bowl victories.

Bud Grant: He took over the losing Minnesota Vikings in 1967. From 1970 through 1980, Grant's pass-happy, bad weather-loving Vikes swept 8 Central Division crowns. In 1 3-year stretch (shades of George Halas), Grant posted 35 wins to only 7 losses. The bad news: Bud lost all 4 Super Bowl games he entered. He's jinxed!

Don Shula: At age 52, one of today's trickiest, winningest mentors, with the highest victory percentage (.708). Shula made a highly controversial switch from Baltimore to Miami in 1970, where his Dolphins have won or tied for 8 Division titles. Shula had a perfect 14-0-0 season record and a Super Bowl triumph in 1972.

Long after his death, memorial banquets in his honor are held across the country. He's the best-recalled, most quoted personality since Knute Rockne of the 1920s. The glittering cup which goes to each year's Super Bowl victor is called the *Vincent T. Lombardi Trophy*.

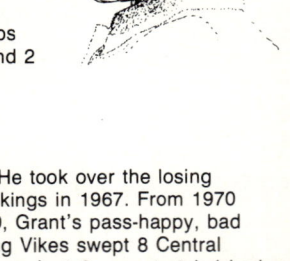

He was, by near-unanimous agreement, the finest pro coach ever to walk onto a field. **Vince Lombardi's** death in 1970 at age 57 (cancer) cut short a phenomenal 10-year run. He turned head coach at Green Bay in 1959, inheriting a demoralized Packer bunch who in 1957-58 had been trounced 19 times in 24 starts. "I've never been on a dog team," Lombardi informed the Packers, "and I have no intention of starting now. We won't do things right once in a while. We'll do them right *all the time.*"

Mr. Football Remembered

Holding cruelly long practice sessions, preaching self-denial and mental discipline, the Brooklyn-born *street-fighter* Lombardi at once converted the Pack into league terrors. The Pack won the NFL West title in **1960.** They won the entire NFL championship in **1961.** They repeated in **1962.** In those 2 years, they were a stunning 22-5-1 in the win-loss-tie column. Lombardi was just warming up.

In **1965** he produced a **third** NFL champ. And a **fourth** in **1966**, going on to wallop Kansas City, 35-10 in the first Super Bowl classic. *Man of steel* Lombardi added a **fifth** title—his third straight NFL banner—in **1967**, capped by another Super Bowl runaway, over Oakland, 33-14.

Gruff, insatiable Lombardi, having overcome every possible challenge at Green Bay, went to the rescue of the Washington Redskins in '69. The Skins hadn't been a contender in 14 seasons. In one year under Lombardi's lash, they became a fired-up contender with a winning percentage.

And then carcinoma took Lombardi. He wasn't given the time to reach the elite 100-games-won coaching circle, finishing at 96 career victories to 34 losses and 6 ties. Considering that he started from point zero in 2 cities, it was amazing—and earned him a place in football mythology.

Lombardi wrote the book on toughness in coaching. Defensive tackle **Henry Jordan** moaned, "He treates us all equal—like dogs." Yet he was beloved by his men. "We all knew that he bled inside for us, that he loved us," said QB **Bart Starr**, the present-day Green Bay coach. At a league meeting, one of the NFL owners spoke of the athletes as *hired hands* who needed to be put in their place regarding contracts and pay. Lombardi, leaping up, roared, **"These aren't truckdrivers—they're artists! Do you understand—artists!"**

Two other Lombardi quotes are everlasting:

"Win a team's heart and they'll follow you anywhere, do the impossible for you."

"The greatest of all accomplishments is not in never failing, but in rising again after you fall."

Teams still use the Lombardi Sweep, Drive Block, Veer Play, Bootleg, Quick Trap and **Linebacker Force.** He was both inspirer and inventor.

Lombardi-taught teams had the following **postseason** record:

W—9 L—1 T—0 Percentage: .900

Combined with his regular-season mark, Lombardi's overall record:

W—105 L—35 T—6 Percentage: .740

His 5 NFL champions won 55, lost only 12 and tied 2.

A magnificent success story ended too soon.

ACTIVE leading coaches

	Coach	Team	Won
1.	**Tom Landry**	*Dallas Cowboys*	**214**
2.	**Don Shula**	*Miami Dolphins*	204
3.	**Bud Grant**	*Minnesota Vikings*	147
4.	**Chuck Noll**	*Pittsburgh Steelers*	131
5.	**Chuck Knox**	*Buffalo Bills*	91

Highest winning percentage:
1. Shula—won 204, lost 83, tied 6: .708
2. Noll—won 131, lost 76, tied 1: .643
3. Grant—won 147, lost 86, tied 5: .641

Note that only 4 present-day team leaders are on the *100 list*—Tom Landry (Dallas), Don Shula (Miami), Bud Grant (Minnesota), Chuck Noll (Pittsburgh).

TOP 10 100-Game Winners

Note that only 4 present-day team leaders are on the 100 list—**Tom Landry** *(Dallas)*, **Don Shula** *(Miami)*, **Bud Grant** *(Minnesota)* and **Chuck Noll** *(Pittsburgh)*.

	Coach	Years	Won	Lost	Tied	Percentage	
1.	**George Halas**	**40**	**326**	**150**	**30**	64	
2.	**Curly Lambeau**	33	234	135	23	60	
3.	**Tom Landry**	22	214	125	6	62	*still active*
4.	**Don Shula**	19	204	83	6	**71**	*still active*
5.	**Paul Brown**	21	170	108	6	60	
6.	**Steve Owen**	23	154	108	17	55	
7.	**Bud Grant**	15	147	86	5	64	*still active*
8.	**Hank Stram**	17	136	100	10	55	
9.	**Weeb Ewbank**	20	134	130	7	49	
10.	**Chuck Noll**	13	131	76	1	64	*still active*

Most **Unusual** Team: Plainfield Teacher's College, 1941. A winning string of scores was called in to the NY Times sports desk. John Chung, Plainfield's quarterback, became a star. The season was nearly over when it was discovered that the Plainfield Teacher's College Team was entirely a hoax dreamed up by Morris Newburger, a Wall Street brokerage house senior partner.

While coaching at Princeton, **Woodrow Wilson** reportedly developed diagrams to chart plays and formations. He was apparently the first ever to use such graphic visual aids.

Worst Current Team: CalTech started in 1893—105 wins, over 300 losses since. Average weight: 160 lbs.

Paul *Bear* Bryant (who got his nickname from once wrestling and beating a carnival bear) said last season, "The experts tell me I'm the youngest 68-year-old in the country.

I'll be around a while longer to whip a few more tails." In 1981, the Alabama U mentor became the winningest coach of all time. He reached his 315th lifetime victory. That surpassed the ancient record of 314 set by **Amos Alonzo Stagg.**

To accomplish 315 victories, Bryant had to last 44 years as a coach. He's Alabama's No. 1 living legend. A commemorative coin with *Bear's* rugged features on it costs $1,250. Sculptures of him go for $4,500.

But the idolized **Bryant** doesn't have the highest win-loss percentage in collegiate ranks. That distinction belongs to **Barry Switzer** of Oklahoma, with a career 90-13-3 win-loss-tie mark, or, .863.

However, neither ***Bear* Bryant** nor **Barry Switzer** holds the supreme coaching record. The No.1 percentage performance still belongs—52 years after his death—to **Kenneth Knute Rockne**, most famous of all grid teachers. In 13 Notre Dame seasons (1918-30), Rockne won an astonishing 105 games, lost but 12 and tied 5—for an .881 percentage. He once knocked off 27 opponents in 29 games. In 1929-30 ***The Rock*** swept 19 games straight without a loss!

Second to **Rockne** comes another Notre Damer, **Frank Leahy**, with an .864 mark. In third place is **Switzer** at .863. After only 10 years of fashioning fine *Boomer Sooner* teams, **Switzer** might be the man to eventually overtake **Rockne.** Close on **Switzer's** heels is **John Robinson** of USC.

Most Victories—Active Coaches

Paul Bryant, *Alabama*	**315**
Bo Schembechler, *Michigan*	163
Joe Paterno, *Penn State*	151
Vince Dooley, *Georgia*	140
Bill Yeoman, *Houston*	139
Jerry Claiborne, *Kentucky*	138
Bobby Bowden, *Florida State*	123
Wayne Hardin, *Temple*	114
Darryl Rogers, *Arizona State*	108
Hayden Fry, *Iowa State*	106

Coach of the Year Award

Coach-of-Year Award—only 3 pigskin professors, ***Bear* Bryant, Darrell Royal** of Texas and **Joe Paterno** of Penn State have twice been selected by the American Football Coaches Association and the Football Writers Association of America for this distinguised award.

Selected by the American Football Coaches Association and the Football Writers Association of America

1935 **Lynn Waldorf,** *Northwestern*
1936 **Dick Harlow,** *Harvard*
1937 **Edward Mylin,** *Lafayette*
1938 **Bill Kern,** *Carnegie Tech*
1939 **Eddie Anderson,** *Iowa*

1940 **Clark Shaughnessy,** *Stanford*
1941 **Frank Leahy,** *Notre Dame*
1942 **Bill Alexander,** *Georgia Tech*
1943 **Amos Alonzo Stagg,** *Pacific*
1944 **Carroll Widdoes,** *Ohio State*
1945 **Bo McMillin,** *Indiana*
1946 **Earl *Red* Blaik,** *Army*
1947 **Fritz Crisler,** *Michigan*
1948 **Bennie Oosterbaan,** *Michigan*
1949 **Bud Wilkinson,** *Oklahoma*

1950 **Charlie Caldwell,** *Princeton*
1951 **Chuck Taylor,** *Stanford*
1952 **Biggie Munn,** *Michigan State*
1953 **Jim Tatum,** *Maryland*
1954 **Henry *Red* Sanders,** *UCLA*
1955 **Duffy Daugherty,** *Michigan State*
1956 **Bowden Wyatt,** *Tennessee*
1957 **Woody Hayes,** *Ohio State*
1958 **Paul Dietzel,** *LSU*
1959 **Ben Schwartzwalder,** *Syracuse*

1960 **Murray Warmath,** *Minnesota*
1961 **Paul *Bear* Bryant,** *Alabama*
1962 **John McKay,** *USC*
1963 **Darrell Royal,** *Texas*
1964 **Frank Broyles,** *Arkansas* and **Ara Parseghian,** *Notre Dame*
1965 **Tommy Prothro,** *UCLA*
1966 **Tom Cahill,** *Army*
1967 **John Pont,** *Indiana*
1968 **Joe Paterno,** *Penn State*
1969 **Bo Schembechler,** *Michigan*

1970 **Charles McClendon,** *LSU* and **Darrell Royal,** *Texas*
1971 **Paul *Bear* Bryant,** *Alabama*
1972 **John McKay,** *USC*
1973 **Paul *Bear* Bryant,** *Alabama*
1974 **Grant Teaff,** *Baylor*
1975 **Frank Kush,** *Arizona State*
1976 **Johnny Majors,** *Pittsburgh*
1977 **Don James,** *Washington*
1978 **Joe Paterno,** *Penn State*
1979 **Earle Bruce,** *Ohio State*

1980 **Vince Dooley,** *Georgia*
1981 **Danny Ford,** *Clemson*

Percentage of Games Won—Active Coaches

(Coaching for a minimum of 5 years in Division 1-A)

Coach	School	Years	Wins	Losses	Ties	Percentage
1. Barry Switzer	*Oklahoma*	9	90	13	3	**.863**
2. **John Robinson**	*USC*	6	59	11	2	.833
3. **Joe Paterno**	*Penn State*	16	151	33	1	.819
4. **Bo Schembechler**	*Michigan*	19	163	41	6	.790
5. **Paul Bryant**	*Alabama*	**37**	**315**	**81**	**17**	.783
6. **Tom Osborne**	*Nebraska*	9	84	23	2	.780
7. **Jackie Sherrill**	*Texas A&M*	6	53	17	1	.754
8. **Dick Crum**	*North Carolina*	8	68	22	2	.750
9. **Carmen Cozza**	*Yale*	17	114	38	3	.745
10. **LaVell Edwards**	*BYU*	10	86	32	1	.727

Winningest Coaches of all time *(by percentage)*

Coach, *College Coached, Tenure*	Years	Won	Lost	Tied	Pct.
1. **Knute K. Rockne** *Notre Dame 1918-30*	13	105	12	5	**.881**
2. **Frank W. Leahy** *Boston Col. 1939-40; Notre Dame 1941-43, 1946-53*	13	107	13	9	.864
3. **George W. Woodruff** *Pennsylvania 1892-01; Illinois 1903; Carlisle 1905*	12	142	25	2	.846
4. **Percy D. Haughton** *Cornell 1899-00; Harvard 1908-16; Columbia 1923-24*	13	96	17	6	.832
5. **Robert R. *Bob* Neyland** *Tennessee 1926-34, 1936-40, 1946-52*	21	173	31	12	.829
6. **Fielding H. *Hurry Up* Yost** *Ohio Wesleyan 1897; Nebraska 1898; Kansas 1899; Stanford 1900; Michigan 1901-23, 1925-26*	29	196	36	12	.828
7. **Charles *Bud* Wilkinson** Oklahoma 1947-63	17	145	29	4	.826
8. **Joseph V. *Joe* Paterno** *Penn State 1966-Present*	15	151	33	1	.818
9. **John B. *Jock* Sutherland** *Lafayette 1919-23; Pittsburgh 1924-38*	20	144	28	14	.812
10. **Robert S. *Bob* Devaney** *Wyoming 1957-61; Nebraska 1962-72*	16	136	30	7	.806
11. **Frank W. Thomas** *Chattanooga 1925-28; Alabama 1931-42, 1944-46*	19	141	33	9	.795
12. **Glenn *Bo* Schembechler** *Miami, Ohio, 1963-68; Michigan 1969-Present*	18	163	41	6	.790
13. **Henry L. Williams** *Army 1891; Minnesota 1900-21*	23	139	34	10	.787
14. **Paul W. *Bear* Bryant** *Maryland 1945; Kentucky 1946-53; Texas A&M 1954-57; Alabama 1958-Present*	**36**	**315**	**81**	17	.783
15. **Gilmour *Gloomy Gil* Dobie** *No. Dakota State 1906-07; Washington 1908-16; Navy 1917-19; Cornell 1920-35; Boston Col. 1936-38*	33	180	45	15	.781
16. **Fred Folsom** *Colorado 1895-99, 1901-02; Dartmouth 1903-06; Colorado 1908-15*	19	106	28	6	.779
17. **Herbert O. *Fritz* Crisler** *Minnesota 1930-31; Princeton 1932-37; Michigan 1938-47*	18	116	32	9	.768
18. **Charles B. *Charley* Moran** *Texas A&M 1909-14; Centre 1919-23; Bucknell 1924-26; Catawba 1930-33*	18	122	33	12	.766
19. **William Wallace Wade** *Alabama 1923-30; Duke 1931-41, 1946-50*	24	171	49	10	.765
20. **Frank Kush** *Arizona State 1958-1979*	22	176	54	1	.764
21. **Daniel E. *Dan* McGugin** *Vanderbilt 1904-17, 1919-34*	30	197	55	19	.762
22. **James *Jimmy* Crowley** *Michigan State 1929-32; Fordham 1933-41*	13	78	21	10	.761

History of Collegiate Football

Collegiate football didn't begin, as often and erroneously reported, with a Princeton-Rutgers clash at New Brunswick, N.J. in 1889.

As far back as 1871, at Harvard, the *Boston Game* was played. In this version, for the first time a ball-packer could run with the pigskin if pursued. In October, 1873, the first Intercollegiate Rules were drafted.

During the 1880s, English Rugby Union rules gave way to a peculiarly American campus sport, as laid down by **Walter *Father of Football* Camp** at Yale. Camp reduced teams from 15 to 11 men. He designed a 7-lineman, 4-back alignment and then a system of downs and yards-to-gain.

The word *gridiron* entered the language in 1882 when chalk stripes were drawn parallel to the goal line, giving the field a grid look. Other innovations of football's formative days were:

1877: The first full uniform was worn by **Leonidas P. Smock** of Princeton. He trotted out to much applause in a jersey with an orange *P*, tight canvas jacket and black knee pants and socks.

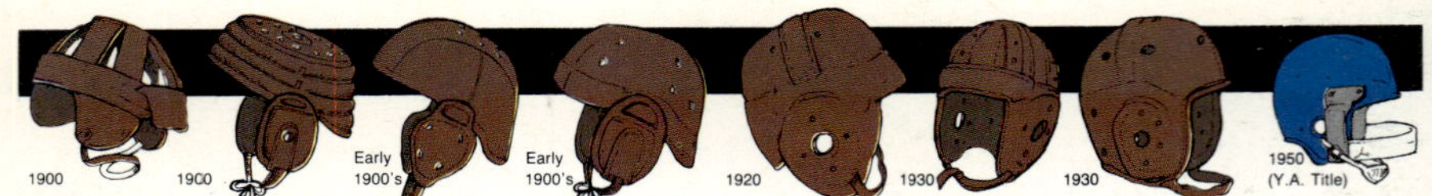

1884: Systemized blocking began with introduction of the *V-trick, or wedge formation*, with large players running interference for a smaller back hiding behind the screen.

The Flying Wedge

tackling dummy and uniform numbers. **Stagg's** 314 career victories stood as the all-time record until **Paul *Bear* Bryant** of Alabama surpassed it in 1981.

Reform era: 1905-1910. To die in action, to give up your life for the old school, was considered noble. So savagely was the game played that 18 collegians died and 159 were seriously injured in 1905. "This must stop," ordered President **Theodore Roosevelt**, "or I'll see that football is ended." Roosevelt summoned Ivy League leaders to the White House and new rules were introduced—slowly. They prevented mass *turtleback* attacking, slugging, hurdling and interlocked interference. Most important

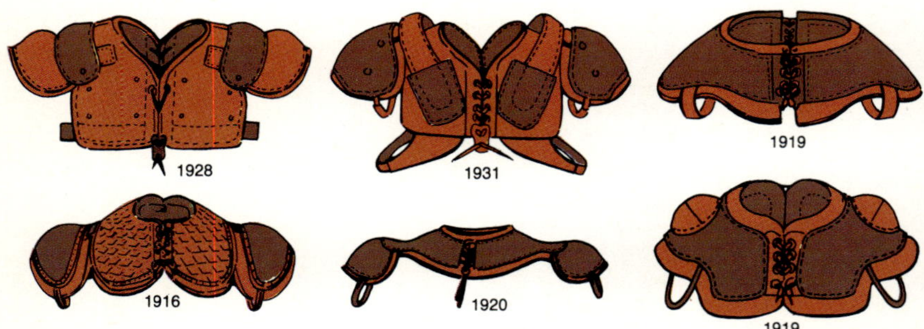

1885: Ending many a fistfight, a referee was named to enforce the rules. The first penalty to be laid down: 5 yards for delay of game.

1889: Walter Camp and **Caspar Whitney** picked the first All-American team, composed exclusively of men from Harvard, Yale and Princeton. Not for 10 years did anyone other than an Easterner make All-American. He was **Clarence Herschberger**, Chicago U's blasting fullback.

Meanwhile, *kickball*, with a touchdown counting as 5 points, was sprouting in the Midwest and Far West. In 1892, Stanford and California U met in the first Pacific Coast collegiate game. In 1895, the Western Conference (later called *Big Ten*) was formed. But the big crowds and rah-rah spirit remained an eastern phenomenon. Harvard opened the first stadium built just for football in 1903.

The legendary innovator: A chunky little genius who lived to be 102 years old, **Amos Alonzo Stagg** did more to change football than anyone in history. **Stagg** said, "Players should meet to discuss strategy before calling signals"—and invented the huddle in 1894. In the next 2 decades, he created the center-snap, man-in-motion, reverses, diagrammed playbook, backfield shifts,

of all, the forward pass was legalized in 1906. *Zipping* the *oblate spheroid* reduced fatalities. So did establishment of a 100-yard field with end zones where a pass could be thrown for a touchdown (now worth 6 points).

Dynasties developed across the nation. Michigan U's dashing *point a minute* teams led by **Willie *The Wisp* Heston** at halfback went 56 games between 1901-1905 without a defeat. Washington U won or tied 63 straight. Other dynasties came along at New York U, under Coach **Chick Meehan**; at Notre Dame, under **Knute Rockne**; at Illinois, with **Red Grange** setting such marks as 4 touchdowns in 12 minutes; at USC, the *Thundering Herd*, under Coach **Howard Jones.**

Other dates worth noting:

1916: Georgia Tech set a scoring mark (never beaten) by crushing Cumberland, 222-0. The Rambling Wrecks scored 32 times.

1920: *Win one for the Gipper* became an historic fight cry when **George Gipp** died of pneumonia in his senior year at Notre Dame. Gipp had run for 4,833 yards on 2,341 rushes, an unmatched feat. On his deathbed, Gipp reportedly told **Coach Knute Rockne**, "When things look bad, tell

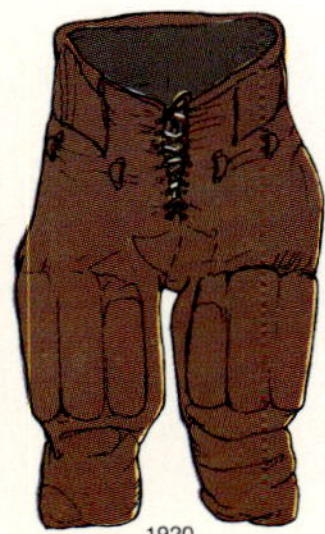

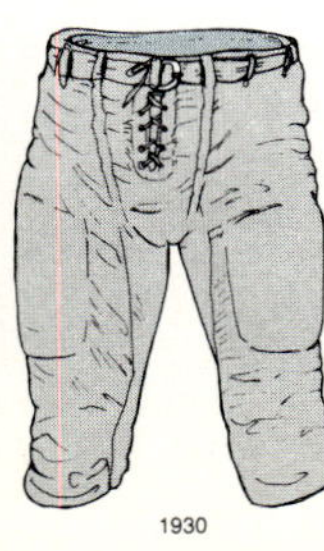

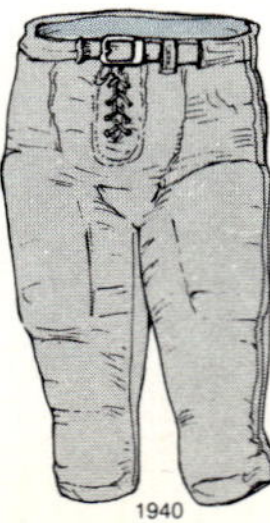

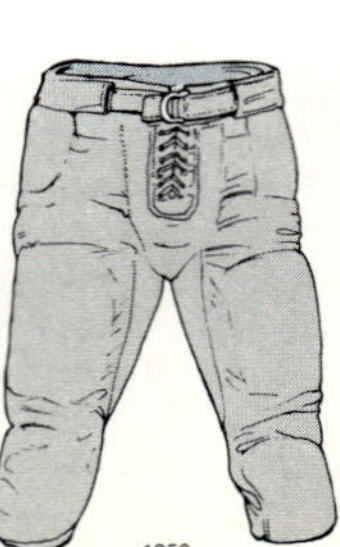

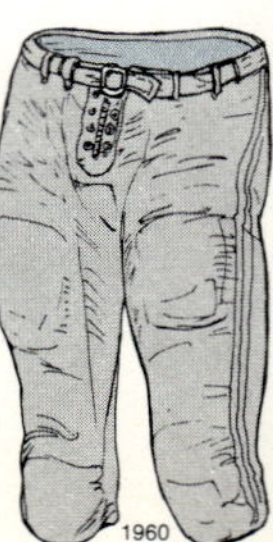

History of Collegiate Football

the boys to go in there and win one for the Gipper.'' And they did!

1924: The *Four Horsemen* backfield of Notre Dame became a legend. The 4 were: **Harry Stuhldreyer**, QB; **Don Miller** and **Jim Crowley**, HBs; **Elmer Layden**, FB. All became coaches and Layden became National Football League commissioner in 1941.

1928: While a Rose Bowl crowd sat aghast, **Roy Riegels**, center for California U, picked up a fumble and ran 64 yards the wrong way. Reigels was tackled short of his own goal by QB **Benny Lom**, but the classic goof-up resulted in a Georgia Tech safety and the Engineers won, 8-7. Fifty years later, Reigels said, ''I've never lived it down.''

1931: Knute Rockne was killed in a plane crash near Bazaar, Kansas. One of the perfectors of the forward pass, *The Rock* had an amazing 105-12-5 record when he died. Under him, Notre Dame had 5 unbeaten seasons and an .881 winning percentage—**the highest ever posted by any coach.**

1939: Tom Harmon, scoring 33 touchdowns in his Michigan career, made **98** the most famous number in college ball since **Red Grange's 77.**

1944: Glen *Mr. Outside* Davis and **Felix *Mr. Inside* Blanchard** led Army to a record high of 56.0 points-per-game. Fans roared in protest when Army wasn't selected for the Rose Bowl.

1958: The first change in scoring rules since 1912 gave the scoring team (touchdown) the option of trying for a 2-point conversion by run or pass from the 3-yard line. Result: Major colleges made the 2-pointers 51.4 per cent of the time.

1970: Yale, playing de-emphasized football, became the only leading major college to win over 600 games.

1981: Oklahoma U's mark of 15 wins, 6 losses and 1 tie, USC's 19-7-0 and Penn State's 12-6-2 in total Bowl-game appearances topped all colleges.

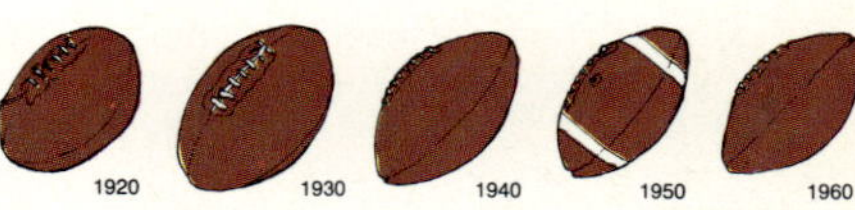

National team champion: Voting bodies sometimes disagree in selecting the annual U.S. champion, but on a concensus basis, Notre Dame leads with 7 titles over the past 45 years. The Fighting Irish spread their national crowns from 1943 through 1977. Alabama and Oklahoma are tied for second place with 5 selections each. Next come Minnesota (which hasn't won since 1960) with 4 picks and USC with 4 picks. Ohio State follows with 3.

Only 6 colleges have won back-to-back national titles: Army, Nebraska, Alabama, Notre Dame, Minnesota and Oklahoma. The only schools to have **twice** won back-to-back collegiate crowns are Oklahoma (1955-56;1974-75) and Alabama (1964-65;1978-79).

Highspots of the College 1981 season: Clemson University of South Carolina was the only major undefeated team in '81, with a spotless overall 12-0 record. This shows how evenly balanced collegiate competition has become.

Coach **Paul *Bear* Bryant** broke **Amos Alonzo Stagg's** longtime record for most coaching victories with his 315th in the final regular-season game.

Iowa University, with its first winning season in 20 years, reached the Rose Bowl, only to be slaughtered by Washington, 28-0—the first Rose Bowl shutout in 28 years.

Marcus Allen continued the string of Southern California University winners of the coveted Heisman Trophy—the 4th USC tailback to be so honored in recent years.

College 1981: How They Finished

At the outset of the '8l season, the strongest favorites for the national championship were Michigan, Texas, USC, Oklahoma, Notre Dame and Penn State. Almost nobody noticed small Clemson University in South Carolina.

So much for the experts.

Clemson's Tigers stunned the country by going unbeaten in 11 regular-season games, the only major team to escape defeat. Led by **Coach Danny Ford**, the Tigers capped the year with a 22-15 win over Nebraska in the Orange Bowl on January 1. Clemson's triumph kept the national title in the south for the fourth straight year—Alabama having taken the crown in 1978-79 and Georgia winning in 1980.

An accepted final regular-season standings list for 1981 *(with number of first place votes)*:

	Team	W	L	T
1	Clemson *(63)*	11	0	0
2	Georgia *(1)*	9	1	0
3	Alabama	9	1	1
4	Nebraska *(1)*	9	2	0
5	SMU	10	1	0
6	Texas	9	1	1
7	Penn St. *(1)*	9	2	0
8	USC	9	2	0
9	Miami	9	2	0
10	Pittsburgh	10	1	0
11	North Carolina	9	2	0
12	Washington	9	2	0
13	Iowa	8	3	0
14	BYU	10	2	0
15	Ohio St.	8	3	0
16	Michigan	8	3	0
17	Arizona St.	9	2	0
18	S. Mississippi	9	1	1
19	UCLA	7	3	1
20	Washington St.	8	2	1

History of Professional Football

Professional football in its first years resembled a battle royal more than a sport with rules. In the early 1890s, steelmill and mineworkers of Pennsylvania, Ohio and West Virginia collided in a savage mixture of rugby and soccer.

Fists could be used. A crunching phalanx of blockers—the *flying wedge*—preceded ball-carriers. Teams ran to 25 men or more. A *touch* (touchdown) counted 4 points.

Uniforms were crude and skimpy until World War I. They consisted at first of a laced canvas shirt, thinly-padded moleskins, *scrum* boots and no helmet. The leather helmet did not evolve until 1910; only a man's shock of hair protected his skull.

When Latrobe, Pennsylvania met Jeannette, Pennsylvania in the first pro game under newly-formed American rules in 1895, players were paid $5 to $10 per game. Recruited college stars demanded more money and game pay shot up. **Pudge Heffelfinger**, a giant All-American lineman at Yale, commanded $500 per game. ***Indian* Jim Thorpe**, of Carlisle and 1912 Olympic Games fame, did equally well. Thorpe was named first president of the American Professional Football Association upon its formation at Canton, Ohio in 1920. "A bunch of men paid $100 each for a franchise," Thorpe related years later, "and in no time at all most of us were broke." Drawing 1,500 or less fans, the failing APFA was reorganized in 1922 as the 18-team National Football League.

Not many of the original 18 franchises survived. Soon to vanish from the scene were such colorful but moneyless outfits as the *Canton Bulldogs, Duluth Eskimos, Oorang Indians, Frankford Yellow Jackets* and *Masillon Tigers* (the latter starring **Knute Rockne**, who went on to become Notre Dame's celebrated coach).

It was **George Halas** of Chicago who saved the game. Halas' Chicago Bears drew well and in 1926 he persuaded **Harold *Red* Grange**, the nationally-idolized *Galloping Ghost* of Illinois U, to turn pro. The Grange-led Bears hit the road, selling out from New York to Los Angeles before crowds of 60,000 to 73,000. Pro football had arrived by way of a coach-promoter born in Austria-Hungary (Halas) and a flashy redheaded halfback born in Forksville, Pennsylvania (Grange)

Then came a number of changes having to do with the playing field, equipment and uniforms. The key events to remember:

1932: In a playoff game, the field was found to be 20 yards too short. The Chicago Bears and Portsmouth Spartans agreed to *move the goal posts from the goal line to the end-zone backline. This was permanently adopted in 1933.*

1934: *A full inch was taken off the girth of the football*, to measure 21½ inches around and 28½ inches in length (still used today). The slimmer ball was better adapted to passing, but it ended the era of the dropkick. The placekick proved easier to control.

1940: *The inbound lines (or hashmarks) were brought out 10 yards from the sidelines*, opening up the game. The Chicago Bears gave the Washington Redskins a famous, record 73-0 shellacking.

1948: Use of a *kicking tee* on kickoffs was legalized.

1954: A new rule requiring the use of *face masks* to end facial injuries was adopted. In 1962, it became illegal to grab the face mask (if done by the defense, an automatic first down is imposed).

1966: The goalposts were standardized in bright gold with uprights extending 20 feet above the crossbar.

Key developments on strategy, passing, manpower, rules, coaching, franchises and television:

1930: Ralph Jones and **Clark Shaughnessy** of the Chicago Bears revived the oldtime **T**-formation. Modified, it swept football.

1933: Forward passing from any point behind the scrimmage line was legalized. It brought on the day of the first 1,000-yards-per-season passers—**Arnie Herber** and **Cecil Isbell** (Green Bay), **Sammy Baugh** (Washington), and **Sid Luckman** (Bears).

1935: The college player-draft system was initiated, ending cutthroat bidding for talent, at least until the NFL-AFL war broke out in 1960.

1936: Coaching from the side line was OK'd after years of penalizing the violators.

1946: The West Coast got pro football when the NFL champion Cleveland Rams moved to Los Angeles; the Rams quickly signed black players, to set a new trend.

1947: Too many boring tied games led to the sudden-death overtime period (or periods) method of settling deadlocks.

1949: Clark *The Magician* Shaughnessy, now with the L.A. Rams, introduced the *third end*, or flanker, to pro ball. His flanker was ***Crazy Legs* Hirsch**, who drove foes daffy with 66 catches and a record 17 touchdown catches in 1951.

History of Professional Football

1966: A 6-year war between the upstart American Football Conference and NFL came to an end with an historic merger. The merger gave the league 24 teams, expanding to 26 by 1968. **Alvin** ***Pete*** **Rozelle** was named commissioner after a long battle lasting through 23 ballots.

1970: Monday night TV football made its debut (ABC), covering 13 games in addition to Sunday broadcasts. Complaints by American wives went unheeded.

1972: *Hashmarks (inbound lines) were moved nearer the field center*—23 yards, 1 foot, 9 inches from the side line. This leaves 18 feet, 6 inches of space (the space between the goal post uprights) in the middle.Which further loosened up the attacking game.

1975: Tampa Bay and Seattle were awarded franchises, bringing the NFL to its present 28-team alignment. The Tampa Bay Buccaneers and Seattle Seahawks proceeded to win only 9 and lose 47 of their games in the first 2 seasons.

Also, a jersey-numbering system begun in 1973 was ratified. Quarterbacks and specialists would carry numbers 1-19; running and defensive backs, 20-49; centers, 50-59; defensive and interior offensive linemen, 60-79; wide receivers and tight ends, 80-89. Only **Jim Otto** of the Oakland Raiders refused to comply. Otto wore 00.

1980-81: Sportswriters named the New Orleans Saints' helmet design (*a French lily*) the worst emblem in the NFL. *Best* honors were split among the L.A. Rams' sweeping horn and the Tampa Bay pirate design.

1982: Joe Montana of the San Francisco 49ers became the nation's new hero when he led his team to Super Bowl victory over the Cincinnati Bengals.

Pro Football's Hall of Fame:

It's easiest to gain admission to the Hall of Fame at Canton, Ohio, if you're a running back. Since the NFL's *Superstar Sanctum* opened in 1961, 24 ball-carriers have been voted in.

Quarterbacks are next most numerous, with 14 selected to date. Ten offensive tackles and 8 offensive ends are enshrined.

The most difficult route to the Hall is to play linebacker or defensive tackle. Only 5 LB's and 5 DT's have reached the Court of Honor. These chosen few:

Linebackers: Dick Butkus, Bill George, Ray Nitschke, Joe Schmidt, Sam Huff

Leo Nomellini

Defensive tackles: Art Donovan, Bob Lilly, Leo Nomellini, Ernie Stautner, Merlin Olson

The quarterback list: Oddly, this includes few modern players. Field generals of the 1920s-50s dominate the Shrine: Paddy Driscoll, Arnie Herber, Ace Parker, Dutch Clark, Sid Luckman, Sammy Baugh, Otto Graham, Norm Van Brocklin, Bob Waterfield. From 1960 to the present, only Johnny Unitas, Bobby Layne, Bart Starr, Y.A. Tittle and George Blanda have been named.

Speedsters: Red Grange, Tony Canadeo, George McAfee, Joe Guyon, Tuffy Leemans, Bill Dudley, Johnny Blood, Charley Trippi, Frank Gifford, Ollie Matson, Hugh McElhenny, Gale Sayers.

(Players must be retired for 5 years before they are eligible for the Hall of Fame, explaining why some recent stars of are missing.)

Biggest man in the Hall? It's 6′8″, 275-pound end Doug Atkins. Would you believe two *midgets* are here? They're 5′11″, 160-pound Paddy Driscoll and 5′10″, 168-pound Ace Parker.

Where do they come from? Pennsylvania leads in most Hall of Famers produced, with 13. Ohio and Texas, with 11 each, come next; Illinois with 10, and California and New York, with 7 each, follow. Members were born as far away as Honduras, Germany, Italy and Canada.

Sammy Baugh

Johnny Unitas

Otto Graham

George Blanda

Don Hutson

Raymond Berry

Ball-toters: Hall of Famers are about equally divided between *bone crushers* and speedy, broken-field artists.

Bone-crushers: Bronko Nagurski, Clarke Hinkle, Ernie Nevers, Ken Strong, Cliff Battles, Jim Thorpe, Marion Motley, Steve Van Buren, Joe Perry, Jim Brown, Jim Taylor.

Bronko Nagurski

Jim Brown

Dream Backfield: From the 110 Hall members, this lineup of super-greats is our choice:

QB's: Sammy Baugh, Johnny Unitas, Otto Graham

RB's: Jim Thorpe, Ernie Nevers, Red Grange, Bronko Nagurski, Jim Brown, Gale Sayers

Receivers: Don Hutson, Elroy *Crazylegs* Hirsch, Tom Fears, Raymond Berry

Evolution of Professional Football

During the 6 decades since its formal beginning in 1921, the NFL has represented a crazy-quilt pattern of membership.

Franchises have hop-skipped about the country under a host of names and owners, a non-stop carnival. What we see today in the NFL's 2-conference lineup of 28 teams didn't solidify into a permanent group until as late as 15 years ago. And even after that came franchise changes.

FOOTBALL/ACCESS provides a decade-by-decade league roster, depicting how the game has developed in 60-odd years.

• Teams with a bullet were champions of the season.

Teams in bold are new teams, or are old teams with new names for that season.

1921 (13 teams)

• Chicago Staleys
Buffalo All-Americans
Akron Pros
Green Bay Packers
Canton Bulldogs
Dayton Triangles
Rock Island Independents
Chicago Cardinals
Cleveland Indians
Rochester Jeffersons
Detroit Heralds
Columbus Panhandles
Cincinnati Celts

1931 (10 teams)

• Green Bay Packers
Portsmouth Spartans
Chicago Bears
Chicago Cardinals
New York Giants
Providence Steamrollers
Stapleton Stapes
Cleveland Indians
Brooklyn Dodgers
Frankford Yellowjackets

Despite 5 dropouts, the NFL didn't diminish. In 1933-34, the **Philadelphia, Pittsburgh** and **Detroit** franchises were born. **Washington** joined in 1937.

1941 (10 teams)

• Chicago Bears
New York Giants
Brooklyn Dodgers
Washington Redskins
Philadelphia Eagles
Pittsburgh Pirates (Steelers)
Green Bay Packers
Detroit Lions
Chicago Cardinals
Cleveland Rams

More dropouts of the '41-'51 decade were replaced by 3 clubs from the rival *All-America Football Conference (AAFC)*: **San Francisco, Baltimore, Cleveland.** Cleveland Rams moved to Los Angeles in 1947.

1951 (12 teams)

• **Los Angeles** Rams
New York Giants
Washington Redskins
Cleveland Browns
Pittsburgh Steelers
Philadelphia Eagles
Chicago Cardinals
Detroit Lions
San Francisco 49ers
Chicago Bears
Green Bay Packers
New York Yanks

A second faction, the *American Football League (AFL)* arrived to explode the game roster to 22 teams. Seven years of war for prestige and talent followed that event. The more-powerful NFL added the **Dallas Cowboys** and **Minnesota Vikings** ('60-'61). Of the 22 clubs, 21 would survive to 1982; the 22nd, the **Dallas Texans**, moved to **Kansas City** as the **Chiefs.**

1961 (22 teams)

• Green Bay Packers (NFL)
New York Giants
Philadelphia Eagles
Cleveland Browns
St. Louis Cardinals
Pittsburgh Steelers
Dallas Cowboys
Washington Redskins
Detroit Lions
Baltimore Colts
Chicago Bears
San Francisco 49ers
Los Angeles Rams
Minnesota Vikings

• **Houston Oilers** (AFL)
Boston Patriots (New England)
New York Titans
Buffalo Bills
Dallas Texans
Denver Broncos
Oakland Raiders
San Diego Chargers

With the NFL-AFL war ended by merger, the modern look arrived—14 more teams than existed only 20 years earlier. Expansion franchises went to **Atlanta** and **Miami** (1966), **New Orleans** (1968) and **Cincinnati** (1968). Pickup of numerous teams from merger with the defunct AFL swelled the combined league.

1971 (26 teams)

• Dallas Cowboys
Miami Dolphins
Cleveland Browns
Minnesota Vikings
Kansas City Chiefs
San Francisco 49ers
Baltimore Colts
New England Patriots
New York Jets
Buffalo Bills
Washington Redskins
Philadelphia Eagles
St. Louis Cardinals
New York Giants
Pittsburgh Steelers
Houston Oilers
Cincinnati Bengals
Oakland Raiders
San Diego Chargers
Denver Broncos
Detroit Lions
Chicago Bears
Green Bay Packers
Los Angeles Rams
Atlanta Falcons
New Orleans Saints

Seattle and **Tampa Bay** were awarded memberships (1976) for an all-time high of 28 teams. This gave the NFL representation in 17 states and the District of Columbia. Only one team which was part of it at the beginning in 1921—the **Green Bay Packers** had survived.

1981-82 (28 teams)

• San Francisco 49ers
Cincinnati Bengals
San Diego Chargers
Miami Dolphins
Buffalo Bills
New York Giants
Dallas Cowboys
Tampa Bay Buccaneers
Washington Redskins
Minnesota Vikings
St. Louis Cardinals
Detroit Lions
Chicago Bears
Atlanta Falcons
Cleveland Browns
Houston Oilers
Los Angeles Rams
Oakland Raiders
Kansas City Chiefs
Denver Broncos
New England Patriots
New York Jets
Philadelphia Eagles
Pittsburgh Steelers
Seattle Seahawks
New Orleans Saints
Green Bay Packers
Baltimore Colts

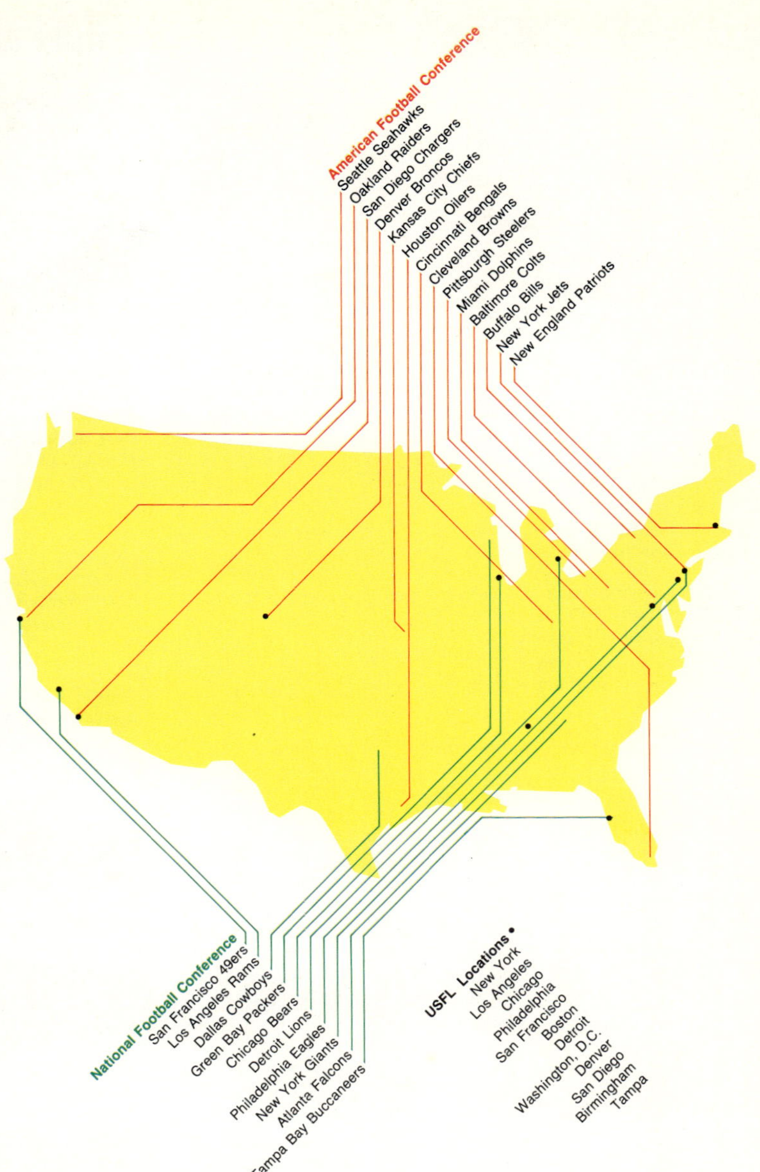

Year 'round football?

In 1983, the newly formed **U.S. Football League** gives us what we've all been waiting for: year-round football. To date the league has 12 teams based in major cities from San Diego to New York City.

The brainchild of **David F. Dixon**, the U.S. Football League has wasted no time in putting down comparisons to the short-lived World Football League. Unlike the WFL, the new league has scheduled an alternate (spring and summer) season, so that it won't be going head-to-head against the firmly established NFL.

The USFL has already gotten a 3-game-per-week commitment from major networks as well as the cable sports channel. And with NFLers and college teams on vacation, they'll have their pick of the major stadia in which to play.

Meanwhile, the *names* aligning themselves with the USFL are adding further credibility. **George Allen** has been tapped as coach and part-owner of one team. **Chester Simmons**, who has held top sports executive posts with major networks, will serve as league commissioner.

Another reason the U.S. League believes in its own success is the wealth of talent available to it: Some 45,000 young men play college football each year, but only 200 are drafted into the pros. It is perhaps one of the richest pools of talent available to any industry, and according to the USFL, certainly big enough to share.

But USFL football will still be football. The new league intends to follow the same rules as the NFL, with some minor exceptions designed to prevent player injuries. The USFL plans to put particular focus on player safety; look for exterior helmet padding and other safety innovations in the league's games.

New York over the years has fielded teams named the **Yankees, Bulldogs, Giants, Yanks** and **Jets.** Los Angeles has known the **Buccaneers, Bulldogs, Dons** and, finally, the **Rams.** Chicago went through the **Staleys, Cardinals, Rockets** and **Bears;** Detroit the **Heralds, Panthers, Wolverines** and, at last, the **Lions.** Cleveland has run the gamut from **Indians, Bulldogs** and **Rams** to today's **Browns.**

College Records

As a Pitt Panther in 1973-76, 180-pound Tony Dorsett survived eye and knee injuries and auto-driving escapades still talked about on campus.

Number 33 was a break-away streak who couldn't be stopped. *Terrific Tony* sped for 1,586 and 1,544 yards in his first 2 seasons. As a senior, he powered Pitt to the national championship with 1,958 yards. His total of 6,082 yards stands today as the most ever run up by a college ball-carrier.

Now an All-Pro with the Dallas Cowboys, he asks to be called Dor-SETT, rather than the DOR-sett of student days. By any pronunciation, he rates among a handful of the super runners in collegiate history.

Yet Dorsett can't flatly be called all time No.1 back. Other contenders for that honor might be:

1920s—Ernie Nevers (Stanford), **George Gipp** (Notre Dame), **Red Grange** (Illinois)

1930s—Tom Harmon (Michigan), **Whizzer White** (Colorado)

1940s—Glenn Davis (Army), **Doak Walker** (SMU)

1950s—Jim Brown (Syracuse), **Billy Cannon** (LSU)

1960s—Gayle Sayers (Kansas), **O.J. Simpson** (USC), **Larry Csonka** (Syracuse)

1970s—Ed Marinaro (Cornell), **Archie Griffin** (Ohio State)

1980s—Herschel Walker (Georgia)

Of that select group of 16, the names of **Red Grange, Glenn Davis, Jim Brown** and **O.J. Simpson** are most prominently mentioned by coaches. Their credentials:

Harold *Red* Grange (Illinois)—None could equal him in the Roaring Twenties when he ran wild in the Big Ten. Three TDs per game were his norm, and against Michigan he once raced for 4 TDs in 12 minutes.

Glenn Davis (Army)—His 59 career touchdowns remain the NCAA record in a tie with Tony Dorsett's, 36 years after he played. Davis's 8.2 per-play gain rushing has never been topped.

Jim Brown (Syracuse)—His 42 points are still the most ever piled up in one game (1956). With brute strength plus racehorse speed, he took Syracuse to the national title.

O.J. Simpson (USC)—Champion of the 80- and 90-yard TD run, he twice led the nation in yards gained rushing.

Among the leading passers in more than 100 years of college play, **Jim McMahon** stands first in the record book. The Brigham Young sharpshooter ended his career in 1981 having chalked up 9,723 yards gained with his arm, beating anything in the books. In passing efficiency (completions, total yards, interceptions), **Danny White** of Arizona State (1971-73), now the big gun of the Dallas Cowboys, is *numero uno.*

But, as with the running backs, this doesn't make McMahon and White the foremost passers of history.

Along with them, the following are generally recognized as the best quarterback-throwers in history:

Sammy Baugh (TCU), **Johnny Lujack** (Notre Dame), **Davey O'Brien** (TCU), **Bob Griese** (Purdue), **John Brodie** (Stanford), **Jerry Rhome** (Tulsa), **Bert Jones** (LSU), **Steve Bartkowski** (California), **Jim Plunkett** (Stanford), **Tommy Kramer** (Rice), **Mark Herrmann** (Purdue), **John Elway** (Stanford).

Four to watch in 1982:

Herschel Walker (Georgia)—With 2 years of eligibility, this 6′2″, 225-pound stud could become the first 7,000-yard career ground-gainer in college annals. May be a legend in the making with his 9.2 speed.

Anthony Carter (Michigan)—A sensational little (5′11″, 160 pounds) pass receiver who has 25 TD grabs and needs only 10 more to break the all-time NCAA record of 34. He has averaged one touchdown for every 4.2 catches.

John Elway (Stanford)—*The Best Gun In The West* has 6,107 yards gained passing, putting him within hailing distance of Jim McMahon's record 9,723. Elway, with 54 aerial touchdowns, will be shooting at McMahon's mark of 84 in 1982.

Dan Marino (Pittsburgh)—Hero of last season's Sugar Bowl game with the winning TD over Georgia in the final 35 seconds, Marino has accumulated 57 touchdowns by air and might be the one to top both McMahon and Elway.

Hail Marcus Allen!

Nicknamed ***Young Juice*** by his USC mates for his physical resemblance to former Trojan ace **O.J. *Orange Juice* Simpson**, 6′2″, 202-pound tailback **Marcus Allen** was the king of amateur football in 1981. Allen won the *best of the year* award (Heisman Trophy) with 441 first-place votes. The runner-up had 152 votes. Allen rushed for 2,342 yards as a senior. He and Simpson are the only NCAA ball-carriers ever to go over 2,000 yards in one season. He had 5 consecutive games of 200 yards-or-more gained and set 12 NCAA records. He led the nation in scoring with 138 points in 11 games.

The Allen saga is all the more remarkable because he started out as a high school quarterback and was fullback blocker at USC as a sophomore. He had to learn to run the tailback position from scratch as a junior.

A high-draft choice of the Oakland Raiders last April, *Young Juice* has fine pro possibilities.

Woody Hayes, Ohio State Coach, 1958: *"When you pass the ball, 3 things can happen—and 2 of them are bad."*

Most in a Game

Points Scored: 43—Jim Brown, Syracuse vs. Colgate, 1956 (6 TDs, 7 PATs)

Touchdowns

Scored: 7—Arnold *Showboat* Boykin, Mississippi vs. Mississippi State, 1951
Passes: 9—Dennis Shaw, San Diego State vs. New Mexico State, 1969
Passes Caught: 6—Tim Delaney, San Diego State vs. New Mexico State, 1969 (16 receptions)

Rushes: 57—Kent Kitzmann, Minnesota vs. Illinois, 1977 (266 yards)

Passes

Completed: 43—Dave Wilson, Illinois vs. Ohio State, 1980 (attempted 69)
43—Rich Campbell, California vs. Florida, 1980 (attempted 53)
Caught: 22—Jay Miller, BYU vs. New Mexico, 1973 (263 yards)

Extra Points by Kicking: 13—Terry Leiweke, Houston vs. Tulsa, 1968 (14 attempts)

Field Goals

Attempted: 8—Frank Fontes, Florida State vs. Wake Forest, 1970 (4 made)
Made: 6—Vince Fusco, Duke vs. Clemson, 1976
(27, 22, 22, 25, 37, 57 yards; 7 attempts)
6—Frank Nester, West Virginia vs. Villanova, 1972
(29, 32, 35, 30, 29, 23 yards; 7 attempts)
6—Charley Gogolak, Princeton vs. Rutgers, 1965
(52, 39, 27, 41, 37, 27 yards; 6 attempts)
Made, 50 Yards or More: 3—Jerry DePoyster, Wyoming vs. Utah, 1966 (54, 54, 52 yards)

Most in a Career

Points Scored: (4 yrs.) 356—Tony Dorsett, Pittsburgh, 1973-76 (59 TDs, 2 PATs)
(3 yrs.) 336— Steve Owens, Oklahoma, 1967-69 (56 TDs)

Touchdowns

Scored: (4 yrs.) 59—Tony Dorsett, Pittsburgh, 1973-76
(55 rushing, 4 pass receptions)
59—Glenn Davis, Army, 1943-46 (43 rushing, 14 pass receptions, 2 punt returns)
Passes: (4 yrs.) 81—Joe Adams, Tennessee State, 1977-80
Passes Caught: 34—Elmo Wright, Houston, 1968-70 (153 receptions)

Rushes: (4 yrs.) 1074—Tony Dorsett, Pittsburgh, 1973-76 (6082 yards)
(3 yrs.) 918—Ed Marinaro, Cornell, 1969-71 (4715 yards)

Passes Completed: (4 yrs.) 717—Mark Herrmann, Purdue, 1977-80 (attempted 1218)
(3 yrs.) 642—Chuck Hixson, SMU, 1968-70 (attempted 1115)

Passes Caught: 261—Howard Twilley, Tulsa, 1963-65 (3343 yards)

Extra Points by Kicking: 171—Vlade Janakievski, Ohio State, 1977-80 (176 attempts)
Per-game record 5.15 by Al Limahelu, San Diego State, 1969-70
(103 in 20)

Field Goals

Attempted: (4 yrs.) 101—Tony Franklin, Texas A&M, 1975-78 (56 made)
101—Dave Jacobs, Syracuse, 1975-78 (53 made)
Made: (4 yrs.) 60—Obed Ariri, Clemson, 1977-80 (92 attempts)
(3 yrs.) 51—Obed Ariri, Clemson, 1978-80 (75 attempts)
Made, 50 Yards or more: 16—Tony Franklin, Texas A&M, 1975-78 (38 attempts)

Farthest in a Game

Most Yards Gained

Rushing: 356—Eddie Lee Ivery, Goergia Tech vs. Air Force, 1978 (26 rushes)
Average, Per Rush: (Min. 20 rushes) 14.8—Hugh McElhenny,
Washington vs. Washington State, 1950 (20 for 296)
(Min. 25 rushes) 13.7—Eddie Lee Ivery,
Georgia Tech vs. Air Force, 1978 (26 for 356)
All-Purpose Rushing: 397—Eric Allen, Michigan State vs. Purdue, 1971
(350 rushing, 47 pass receiving)
Passing: 621—Dave Wilson, Illinois vs. Ohio State, 1980 (completed 43 of 69)
Total Offense: 599—Virgil Carter, Brigham Young vs. Texas-El Paso,
1966 (86 rushing, 513 passing)
Interception Returns: 181—Charles Phillips, USC vs. Iowa, 1974 (2 interceptions)
Average, Per Punt: (Min. 10) 53.6—Jim Benien, Oklahoma State vs. Colorado, 1971
(10 for 536)

Longest Field Goal Made: 67—Joe Williams, Wichita State vs. Southern Illinois, 1978
67—Steve Little, Arkansas vs. Texas, 1977
67—Russell Erxleben, Texas vs. Rice, 1977

Farthest in a Career

Most Yards Gained

Rushing: (4 yrs.) 6082—Tony Dorsett, Pittsburgh, 1973-76 (1074 rushes)
Average, Per Rush: (Min. 300 rushes) 8.26—Glenn Davis, Army, 1943-46 (358 for 2957)
(Min. 500 rushes) 7.09—Billy Sims, Oklahoma, 1975-79 (538 for 3813) (Min. 650 rushes) 6.13—Archie Griffin, Ohio State, 1972-75
(845 for 5177)
All-Purpose Rushing: (4 yrs.) 6615—Tony Dorsett, Pittsburgh, 1973-76
(6082 rushing, 406 receiving, 127 kickoff returns, 1120 plays)
Passing: (4 yrs.) 9188—Mark Herrmannn, Purdue, 1977-80
Total Offense: (4 yrs.) 8444—Mark Herrmann, Purdue 1977-80
(9188 passing, minus 744 rushing)
Interception Returns: 470—John Provost, Holy Cross, 1972-74 (27 interceptions)
Average, Per Punt: (Min. 175) 44.7—Ray Guy, Southern Mississippi., 1970-72
(200 for 8934)

Albie Booth, 135-pound Yale halfback, 1929, (before Penn game): *"Keep in mind, the other guys put on their pants the same way we do—one leg at a time."*

Bronko Nagurski when arriving at Minnesota U as a massive freshman and asked what position he played: *"All of them."*

College Records

Most—Team in a Game

Points	
Scored:	103—Wyoming vs. Northern Colorado (0), 1949 (15 TDs, 13 PATs)
Scored, Against a Major College Opponent:	100—Houston vs. Tulsa (6), 1968 (14 TDs, 13 PATs, 1FG)
Scored, Both Teams:	124—Oklahoma (82) & Colorado (42), 1980
Passes	
Completed:	43—Illinois vs. Ohio State, 1980 (attempted 69) 43—California vs. Florida, 1980 (attempted 53)
Completed, Both Teams:	63—San Diego State (33) and North Texas State (30), (attempted 124)
Touchdown:	10—San Diego State vs. New Mexico State, 1969
Intercepted:	11 by Brown, vs. Rhode Island, 1949 (136 yards)
Intercepted and Fumbles Recovered:	13—by Georgia Tech vs. Georgia, 1951 (8 passes intercepted, 5 fumbles recovered)
Fumbles, Both Teams:	27—Wichita State (17) and Florida State (10), 1969 (lost 17)

Most—Team in a Season

Points	
Per Game:	56.0 Army, 1944 (504 in 9)
Scored:	560—Brigham Young, 1980 (12 games)
Allowed and Allowed Per Game:	544 and 49.5—Texas-El Paso, 1973 (11 games)
Biggest Deficit Overcome by a Winning Team:	27—Utah (28), Arizona (27), 1973 (trailed 27-0 with 14:42 left) 27—Davidson (42), East Carolina (27), 1969 (trailed 27-0 at halftime)
Highest Scoring Tie Game:	48-48—San Jose State and Utah State, 1979
Passes	
Touchdown, Per Game:	4.3—San Diego State, 1969 (43 in 10)
Intercepted Per Game:	4.13—by Pennsylvania, 1940 (33 in 8)
Touchdowns on Interception Returns:	7—Tennessee, 1971
Fumbles Lost:	39—Texas Southern, 1977 (fumbled 68 times)

Most—Team

Consecutive	
Victories:	47—Oklahoma, 1953-57
Games Without Defeat:	48—Oklahoma, 1953-57 (1 tie)
Losses:	28—Virginia, 1958-60 28—Kansas State, 1945-48

Farthest—Team in a Game

Yards	
Gained Rushing:	758—Oklahoma vs. Colorado, 1980 (73 rushes)
Gained Rushing, Both Teams:	1039—Lenoir Rhyne (837) and Davidson (202), 1975 (111 rushes)
Gained Passing:	698—Tulsa vs. Idaho State, 1967 (completed 39 of 62)
Gained Passing, Both Teams:	911—Texas-El Paso (510) and New Mexico (401), 1967 (103 attempts)
Gained, Total Offense:	875—Oklahoma vs. Colorado, 1980 (758 rushing, 117 passing; 80 plays)
Gained, Total Offense, Both Teams:	1347—Oklahoma (785) and Kansas State (562), 1971 (168 plays)
Penalized, Both Teams:	421—Grambling (16 for 216 yards) and Texas Sothern (17 for 205 yards), 1977

Farthest—Team in a Season

Yards	
Gained Per Game, Rushing:	472.4 Oklahoma, 1971 (5196 in 11)
Gained Passing:	4918—Brigham Young, 1980 (12 games)
Gained Per Game, Passing:	409.8—Brigham Young, 1980 (4918 in 12)
Gained Per Game, Total Offense:	566.5—Oklahoma, 1971 (6232 in 11)
Highest Average Gained Per Play, Total Offense:	7.92—Army, 1945 (526 for 4146)

Fewest—Team in a Season

Points Allowed Per Game:	0.0—Tennessee, 1939 (10 games); Duke, 1938 (9 games)
Yards Allowed Per Game:	17.0—Penn State, 1947, (153 in 9)
Average Yards Allowed Per Rush:	0.64—Penn State, 1947 (240 for 153)
Yards Allowed Per Game:	13.1—Penn State, 1938 (105 in 8)
Yards Allowed Per Game:	69.9—Santa Clara, 1937 (559 in 8)

Best Single-Game Performances, Individual

Longest Plays:	Since 1941, official maximum length of all plays fixed at 100 yards
Kickoff Returns:	Since 1941, 135 players (including 12 in 1980, have returned kickoffs 100 yards
Interception Returns:	Since 1941, 42 players have returned interceptions 100 yards. The most recent:

Yards	Player, Team, (Opponent), Year
100	Marty Murray, Indiana State (Southern Illinois), 1977
100	Putt Choate, SMU (Tulane), 1977
100	Dave Petway, Northern Illinois (Southern Illinois), 1977
100	Tom Pridemore, West Virginia (Penn State), 1977

Longest Passing Team

Yards	Passer-Receiver, Team, (Opponent), Year
99	Cris Collinsworth-Derrick Gaffney, Florida (Rice), 1977

Punts

9	Pat Brady, Nevada-Reno (Loyola, Cal.), 1950
96	George O'Brien, Wisconsin (Iowa), 1952

All-Time Winningest 1-A Teams

(Classified as Division 1 for the last 15 years. Won-lost-tied record includes bowl games.)

By Number of Victories:

	Wins		Wins		Wins
Yale	**718**	Alabama	585	Dartmouth	534
Harvard	643	Penn State	568	Army	518
Princeton	642	Ohio State	562	Navy	506
Michigan	623	Nebraska	557	Minnesota	500
Notre Dame	621	Oklahoma	554	LSU	496
Pennsylvania	617	USC	544	Michigan State	455
Texas	605	Tennessee	536	Arizona State	364

By Percentage:

**Ties computed as half won and half lost.*

		Yrs.	Won	Lost	Tied	Pct.*	Bowl Games W	L	T
1.	Notre Dame	93	621	172	39	**.770**	7	3	0
2.	Yale	**109**	**718**	203	53	.764	0	0	0
3.	Michigan	102	632	209	31	.743	6	7	0
4.	Alabama	87	585	199	42	.734	18	14	3
5.	Texas	89	605	219	30	.72	15	11	2
6.	USC	89	544	201	48	.716	**20**	7	0
7.	Oklahoma	87	554	207	49	.714	16	6	1
8.	Ohio State	92	562	224	48	.703	7	9	0
9.	Penn State	95	568	255	39	.682	12	6	2
10.	Tennessee	85	536	239	45	.681	12	12	0
11.	Nebraska	92	557	267	39	.668	11	9	0
12.	Army	92	518	263	49	.654	1	0	0
13.	LSU	88	496	268	42	.641	10	11	1
14.	Arizona State	67	364	201	21	.639	6	4	1
15.	Minnesota	98	500	276	40	.637	1	2	0

National Champions, from 1936

(Based on Associated Press poll of sportswriters, United Press International poll of coaches, Football Writers' Association of America's Grantland Rice Award and National Football Foundation and Hall of Fame's MacArthur Bowl Award.)

1936	Minnesota	1941	Minnesota	1946	Notre Dame
1973	Pittsburgh	1942	Ohio State	1947	Notre Dame
1938	Texas Christian	1943	Notre Dame	1948	Michigan
1939	Texas A&M	1944	Army	1949	Notre Dame
1940	Minnesota	1945	Army		

	AP	UPI	FWAA	NFF-HF
1950	Oklahoma	Oklahoma		
1951	Tennessee	Tennessee		
1952	Michigan State	Michigan State		
1953	Maryland	Maryland		
1954	Ohio State	UCLA	UCLA	
1955	Oklahoma	Oklahoma	Oklahoma	
1956	Oklahoma	Oklahoma	Oklahoma	
1957	Auburn	Ohio State	Ohio State	
1958	Louisiana State	Lousiana State	Iowa	
1959	Syracuse	Syracuse	Syracuse	Syracuse
1960	Minnesota	Minnesota	Mississippi	Minnesota
1961	Alabama	Alabama	Ohio State	Alabama
1962	USC	USC	USC	USC
1963	Texas	Texas	Texas	Texas
1964	Alabama	Alabama	Arkansas	Notre Dame
1965	Alabama	Michigan State	Michigan State & Alabama (tie)	Michigan State
1966	Notre Dame	Notre Dame	Notre Dame	Notre Dame & Michigan State (tie)
1967	USC	USC	USC	USC
1968	Ohio State	Ohio State	Ohio State	Ohio State
1969	Texas	Texas	Texas	Texas
1970	Nebraska	Texas	Nebraska	Ohio State & Texas (tie)
1971	Nebraska	Nebraska	Nebraska	Nebraska
1972	USC	USC	USC	USC
1973	Notre Dame	Alabama	Notre Dame	Notre Dame
1974	Oklahoma	USC	USC	USC
1975	Oklahoma	Oklahoma	Oklahoma	Oklahoma
1976	Pittsburgh	Pittsburgh	Pittsburgh	Pittsburgh
1977	Notre Dame	Notre Dame	Notre Dame	Notre Dame
1978	Alabama	USC	Alabama	Alabama
1979	Alabama	Alabama	Alabama	Alabama
1980	Georgia	Georgia	Georgia	Georgia
1981	Clemson	Clemson	Clemson	Clemson

College Records

Annual Champions, Rushing

Year Player, Team	Plays	Yards
1937 Byron *Whizzer* White, Colorado	181	1121
1938 Len Eshmont, Fordham	132	831
1939 John Polanski, Wake Forest	137	882
1940 Al Ghesquiere, Detroit	146	957
1941 Frank Sinkwich, Georgia	209	1103
1942 Rudy Mobley, Hardin-Simmons	187	1281
1943 Creighton Miller, Notre Dame	151	911
1944 Wayne *Red* Williams, Minnesota	136	911
1945 Bob Fenimore, Oklahoma State	142	1048
1946 Rudy Mobley, Hardin-Simmons	227	1262
1947 Wilton Davis, Hardin-Simmons	193	1173
1948 Fred Wendt, Texas-El Paso	184	1570
1949 John Dottley, Mississippi	208	1312
1950 Wilford White, Arizona State	199	1502
1951 Ollie Matson, San Francisco	245	1566
1952 Howie Waugh, Tulsa	164	1372
1953 J.C. Caroline, Illinois	194	1256
1954 Art Luppino, Arizona	179	1359
1955 Art Luppino, Arizona	209	1313
1956 Jim Crawford, Wyoming	200	1104
1957 Leon Burton, Arizona State	117	1126
1958 Dick Bass, Pacific	205	1361
1959 Pervis Atkins, New Mexico State	130	971
1960 Bob Gaiters, New Mexico State	197	1338
1961 Jim Pilot, New Mexico State	191	1278
1962 Jim Pilot, New Mexico State	208	1247
1963 Dave Casinelli, Memphis State	219	1016
1964 Brian Piccolo, Wake Forest	252	1044
1965 Mike Garrett, USC	267	1440
1966 Ray McDonald, Idaho	259	1329
1967 O.J. Simpson, USC	266	1415
1968 O.J. Simpson, USC	355	1709
1969 Steve Owens, Oklahoma	358	1523

Beginning in 1970, ranked on per-game (instead of total) yards

Year	Player, Team	Cl.	Games	Plays	Yards	Avg.
1970	Ed Marinaro, Cornell	Jr.	9	285	1425	158.3
1971	Ed Marinaro, Cornell	Sr.	9	356	1881	209.0
1972	Pete VanValkenberg, BYU	Sr.	10	232	1386	138.6
1973	Mark Kellar, Northern Illinois	Sr.	11	291	1719	156.3
1974	Louie Giammona, Utah State	Jr.	10	329	1534	153.4
1975	Ricky Bell, USC	Jr.	11	357	1875	170.5
1976	Tony Dorsett, Pittsburgh	Sr.	11	338	1948	177.1
1977	Earl Campbell, Texas	Sr.	11	267	1744	158.5
1978	Billy Sims, Oklahoma	Jr.	11	231	1762	160.2
1979	Charles White, USC	Sr.	10	293	1803	180.3
1980	George Rogers, South Carolina	Sr.	11	297	1781	161.9
1981	Marcus Allen, USC	Sr.	11	403	2342	212.9

Collegiate Football: Factories for the Pros

Alumni who take pride in the number of athletes who graduate from their alma maters to become National Football Leaguers should appreciate the following information:

Which university currently produces the most pro players?

It isn't—as you might suspect—Notre Dame, the most gridiron-conscious school in America. Nor is it mighty Michigan of the Big 10, Eastern hotshot Penn State or Alabama's noted pipeline to the pros.

The most prolific producer is the University of Southern California, with 48 former Trojans on NFL veteran rosters in the 1981 season. Oklahoma's Sooners and Penn State are tied for second with 36 each. Colorado U is a surprising 3rd with 35.

Among USC's many campus-to-NFL players are **Anthony Munoz**, Cincinnati tackle; **Ricky Bell** and **Jim Obradovich** of Tampa Bay; **Brad Budde** of Kansas City; **Marvin Powell**, New York Jets; **Ron Yary** and **Dennis Johnson** of Minnesota; **Lynn Cain** of Atlanta; **Vince Evans**, Chicago Bears; and **Charlie Young**, San Francisco.

The following is a selection of schools that, in the last few years, have supplied 10 or more players to the Pros.

PAC-10 CONFERENCE

USC	48
UCLA	25
California	20
Washington	16
Arizona State	14
Stanford	14
Washington State	10
Oregon	10

BIG 8 CONFERENCE

Oklahoma	36
Colorado	35
Nebraska	27
Kansas	19
Missouri	14
Oklahoma State	11
Kansas State	10

BIG 10 CONFERENCE

Michigan	23
Ohio State	21
Michigan State	15
Purdue	15
Minnesota	10
Wisconsin	10

SOUTHWEST CONFERENCE

Texas A&M	20
Baylor	17
Texas	16
Arkansas	13

SOUTHEASTERN CONFERENCE

Alabama	21
Florida	16
Kentucky	15
Tennessee	12
Louisiana State	11

ATLANTIC COAST CONFERENCE

Georgia Tech	15
Clemson	14
Maryland	11
North Carolina	10

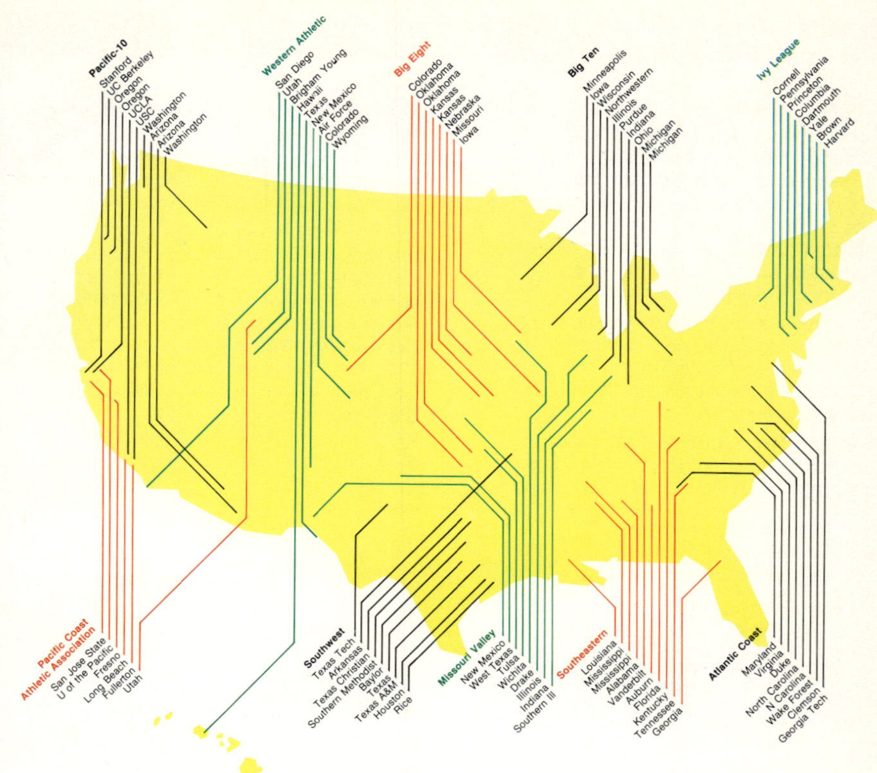

Top Collegiate Teams, 1977-81

As the chart below shows, the entire U.S. is represented in a ranking of the winningest teams over the past 5 years.

In the first 10 are schools from the South, Rocky Mountains, Plains states, Southwest, Pacific Coast, Midwest and East.

Alabama ranks tops with 49 victories in 55 regular-season contests. Such usual powerhouses as Georgia and Notre Dame have slipped to 16th and 20th places, respectively.

Oklahoma U leads everyone in rushing offense and is 4th behind BYU, Nebraska and Nevada-Las Vegas in total offense.

Top Collegiate Team Rankings

Regular Season Only
1977 through 1981

	Team	W	L	T	%	National Ranking, Offense Rush	Pass	*T.O.	Score
1	Alabama	49	5	1	.900	3	127	9	6
2	BYU	50	8	0	.862	126	1	1	1
3	Pittsburgh	46	8	1	.845	88	10	19	7
4	Penn State	46	9	0	.836	27	44	16	10
5	Central Michigan	45	9	1	.827	4	118	20	23
5	Oklahoma	45	9	1	.827	1	137	4	2
7	USC	45	9	2	.821	8	45	7	11
8	Michigan	45	10	0	.818	7	82	11	8
8	Nebraska	45	10	0	.818	2	90	2	3
10	Texas	44	10	1	.809	20	86	31	20
10	Ohio State	44	10	1	.809	6	56	8	4
12	Yale	37	8	2	.808	42	75	57	39
13	Florida State	44	11	0	.800	85	13	27	12
14	Clemson	43	11	1	.791	19	79	26	35
15	Arkansas	43	12	0	.782	14	81	22	13
16	Georgia	41	13	1	.755	25	109	50	34
18	Washington	41	14	0	.745	57	55	49	14
18	McNeese State	40	13	2	.745	18	128	67	40
20	North Carolina	39	14	2	.727	15	93	30	28
21	Notre Dame	39	15	1	.718	37	33	25	25
22	Houston	38	16	1	.700	9	108	21	31
23	Arizona State	39	17	0	.696	24	17	5	5
25	Rutgers	37	18	0	.673	60	69	71	51

*Total Offense

College Records

HEISMAN MEMORIAL TROPHY: The premier award in college sports, the *Heisman* dates back to 1935 and is named for **John W. Heisman** (noted coach from 1891-1927 at Penn, Georgia Tech and Rice). It goes to the footballer considered by the sponsoring *New York Downtown Athletic Club* to be, in its words, "the most outstanding in the United States."

Controversy surrounds the Heisman. The chief criticism is that only 2 non-backfield men have ever won the trophy. However all players covet the honor, which brings overnight celebrity.

First winner: Jay Berwanger, Chicago U back (one of the few winners who didn't turn pro).

Most recent winner: Marcus Allen, USC tailback, 1981.

Lineman winners: Larry Kelley, Yale end of 1936, and Leon Hart, Notre Dame end of 1949, are the only up-front men ever to take the award.

Winningest colleges: Notre Dame, with 6 recipients, holds more Heismans than any school, with wins by **Angelo Bertelli, Johnny Lujack, Leon Hart, Johnny Lattner, Paul Hornung** and **John Huarte.** Ohio State ranks second with 5 winners, USC third with 4. **Archie Griffin**, Ohio State's great back (1974-75) is the only man to have won the Heisman twice. The complete list of winners:

Year	Player, College, Position
1935	Jay Berwanger, Chicago, HB
1936	Larry Kelley, Yale, E
1937	Clint Frank, Yale, HB
1938	Davey O'Brien, TCU, QB
1939	Nile Kinnick, Iowa, HB
1940	Tom Harmon, Michigan, HB
1941	Bruce Smith, Minnesota, HB
1942	Frank Sinkwich, Georgia, HB
1943	Angelo Bertelli, Notre Dame, QB
1944	Les Horvath, Ohio State, QB
1945	*Doc Blanchard, Army, FB
1946	Glenn Davis, Army, HB
1947	John Lujack, Notre Dame, QB
1948	*Doak Walker, SMU, HB
1949	Leon Hart, Notre Dame, E
1950	*Vic Janowicz, Ohio State, HB
1951	Dick Kazmaier, Princeton, HB
1952	Billy Vessels, Oklahoma, HB
1953	John Lattner, Notre Dame, HB
1954	Alan Ameche, Wisconsin, FB
1955	Howard Cassady, Ohio State, HB
1956	Paul Hornung, Notre Dame, QB
1957	John Crow, Texas A&M, HB
1958	Pete Dawkins, Army, HB
1959	Billy Cannon, LSU, HB
1960	Joe Bellino, Navy, HB
1961	Ernie Davis, Syracuse, HB
1962	Terry Baker, Oregon State, QB
1963	*Roger Staubach, Navy, QB
1964	John Huarte, Notre Dame, QB
1965	Mike Garrett, USC, HB
1966	Steve Spurrier, Florida, QB
1967	Gary Beban, UCLA, QB
1968	O.J. Simpson, USC, HB
1969	Steve Owens, Oklahoma, HB
1970	Jim Plunkett, Stanford, QB
1971	Pat Sullivan, Auburn, QB
1972	Johnny Rodgers, Nebraska, FL
1973	John Cappellitti, Penn State, HB
1974	*Archie Griffin, Ohio State, HB
1975	Archie Griffin, Ohio State, HB
1976	Tony Dorsett, Pittsburgh, HB
1977	Earl Campbell, Texas, HB
1978	*Billy Sims, Oklahoma, HB
1979	Charles White, USC, HB
1980	George Rogers, So. Carolina, HB
1981	Marcus Allen, USC, TB

**Juniors (all others seniors).*

OUTLAND TROPHY: Given to the outstanding interior lineman of the year by the *Football Writers Association of America*. The *Outland* puts the national spotlight on the men in *the pits* and has been won a record 4 times by Oklahoma U linemen.

Most famous recipients: Alex Karras, Iowa tackle, 1957, and **Merlin Olsen,** Utah State tackle, 1961, both now TV/movie performers. Complete list:

Year	Player, College, Position
1946	George Connor, Notre Dame, T
1947	Joe Steffy, Army, G
1948	Bill Fischer, Notre Dame, G
1949	Ed Bagdon, Michigan State, G
1950	Bob Gain, Kentucky, T
1951	Jim Weatherall, Oklahoma, T
1952	Dick Modzelewski, Maryland, T
1953	J.D. Roberts, Oklahoma, G
1954	Bill Brooks, Arkansas, G
1955	Calvin Jones, Iowa, G
1956	Jim Parker, Ohio State, G
1957	Alex Karras, Iowa, T
1958	Zeke Smith, Auburn, G
1959	Mike McGee, Duke, T
1960	Tom Brown, Minnesota, G
1961	Merlin Olson, Utah State, T
1962	Bobby Bell, Minnesota, T
1963	Scott Appleton, Texas, T
1964	Steve DeLong, Tennessee, T
1965	Tommy Nobis, Texas, G
1966	Loyd Phillips, Arkansas, T
1967	Ron Yary, USC, T
1968	Bill Stanfill, Georgia, T
1969	Mike Reid, Penn State, DT
1970	Jim Stillwagon, Ohio State, MG
1971	Larry Jacobson, Nebraska, DT
1972	Rich Glover, Nebraska, MG
1973	John Hicks, Ohio State, OT
1974	Randy White, Maryland, DE
1975	Leroy Selmon, Oklahoma, DT
1976	Ross Browner, Notre Dame, DE
1977	Brad Shearer, Texas, DT
1978	Greg Roberts, Oklahoma, G
1979	Jim Ritcher, N.C. State, C
1980	Mark May, Pittsburgh, OT
1981	Dave Rimington, Nebraska, T

Johnny McKay, USC Coach, 1973 (to his squad before a Notre Dame game): *"It's an immense game, all right, but keep in mind that there are 600 million Chinese who don't give a damn whether we win or lose."*

Red Sanders, UCLA Coach, 1954 (when students surrounded his house to serenade him): *"Watch out, one of them's got a rope."*

VINCE LOMBARDI AWARD: goes to the outstanding lineman (any line position) of the year. Newest of the awards, the *Lombardi* dates to 1970. The honored players:

Year	Player, College, Position
1970	Jim Stillwagon, Ohio State, MG
1971	Walt Patulski, Notre Dame, DE
1972	Rich Glover, Nebraska, MG
1973	John Hicks, Ohio State, OT
1974	Randy White, Maryland, DT
1975	Leroy Selmon, Oklahoma, DT
1976	Wilson Whitley, Houston, DT
1977	Ross Browner, Notre Dame, DE
1978	Bruce Clark, Penn State, DT
1979	Brad Budde, USC, G
1980	Hugh Green, Pittsburgh, DE
1981	Kenneth Sims, Texas, DT

Benny Owen, Oklahoma U Coach, 1908: *"Think fight, talk fight, always fight."*

Do Heisman, Outland and Lombardi winners always earn professional stardom? Sometimes. As witness Doak Walker, Alan Ameche, Paul Hornung, Roger Staubach, O.J. Simpson, Billy Sims, Earl Campbell, Tony Dorsett, Ron Yary, Tommy Nobis, Merlin Olsen, Leroy Selmon, Hugh Green, Randy White.

Paul *Bear* Bryant, Alabama Coach, 1974: *Show me a football coach who has time to shoot good golf and I'll show you a (censored) coach."*

ALL-AMERICAN SELECTIONS: Because they were the first colleges to field varsity teams, beginning in the 1880s, Yale and Harvard have placed more men on All-American lists than any other schools. More recently, Notre Dame and Michigan had the best records. The top 10 standings (number of selections in parentheses):

1. **Yale** (100)
2. **Harvard** (89)
3. **Notre Dame** (78)
4. **Princeton** (65)
5. **Michigan** (52)
6. **Pennsylvania** (47)
7. **Ohio State** (47)
8. **USC** (46)
9. **Oklahoma** (40)
10. **Army** (37)

TRIPLE ALL-AMERICANS: One of the rarest feats is to land on a concensus A-A team 3 times. In the old days, **Red Grange**, Illinois, **Wes Fesler**, Ohio State, **Doc Blanchard** and **Glenn Davis**, Army, did it. Another super-hero was **Doak Walker** of Southern Methodist U. Since 1970, only 4 players have made All-American 3 times: **Ken MacAfee**, Notre Dame tight end (1975-76-77); **Jerry Robinson**, UCLA linebacker (1976-77-78); **Hugh Green**, Pittsburgh defensive lineman (1978-79-80); **Kenny Easley**, UCLA defensive end (1978-79-80).

Collegiate Groups

Through the years, fanciful and flashy names have been attached to certain college teams and units within teams.

Iron Men of Sewanee: An 1899 team of 14 men from a tiny Tennessee mountain school that played 5 games in 6 days against big colleges spread over 3,000 miles and won them all.

Wonder Teams: Coach Andy Smith's unbeaten 1920-24 squads at California U won 44 games, tied 4.

Praying Colonels: Pride of the South from rural Centre College, Kentucky, who upset mighty Harvard in 1921, 6-0. The nickname came from a team prayer issued before every game.

Lonely End: Army's unique wingman of 1957, **Bill Carpenter.** He split far out, never joined the cadets' huddle and mysteriously received the signal call. Poems were written to the *Lonely End.*

Team Named Desire: Navy's 1954 crew which after a 6 wins, 2 losses record was given no chance against Army, but surprised everyone by winning a thriller, 27-20.

Sizeable Seven: Kingsize Syracuse line of 1969. Behind this unit Syracuse won 11 straight and received votes as national champion.

Vow Boys: Stanford's freshman squad of 1933 which vowed never to lose to the USC Trojans in their college career—and never did. Starring All-Americans **Bobby Grayson, Bob Reynolds** and **Monk Moscrip.**

Wow Boys: Stanford's winning 1941 Rose Bowl team (21-13 over Nebraska), which (with **Frankie Albert** at quarterback) revived and popularized the **T**-formation.

Thundering Herd: USC's dazzling teams of the 1925-40 era. Coached by **Howard *Headman* Jones**, the Herd won 5 times in the Rose Bowl and produced an astonishing number of All-Americans: backs **Morley Drury, Ernie Pinckert, Gaius Shaver, Cotton Warburton, Orv Mohler, Mort Kaer** and **Grenny Lansdell,** and 11 All-American linemen.

Four Horsemen: Of Notre Dame. (See *History*).

Seven Blocks of Granite: Fordham U's rugged defensive line of 1935-6 which, in '36, allowed not one touchdown. (**Vince Lombardi**, later a revered pro coach, played guard on the *Blocks*.)

Chinese Bandits: Louisiana State's hot pass-intercepting defensive backfield unit of 1958, which helped LSU to the national championship.

Collegiate 1st's

1st rules: Formulated at a meeting held in October, 1873, in New York City and attended by representatives of Princeton, Yale, Rutgers and Columbia.

1st goal posts: Used in a contest between Harvard and McGill University of Montreal at Cambridge, Massachusetts. in 1874. An admission fee was charged—another collegiate football **1st.** Old records show that the money collected was used to lavishly entertain the visiting Canadians.

1st tackling dummy: A gymnasium mat sewed together by pioneer coach **Amos Alonzo Stagg** at Yale University in 1889.

1st uniform numbers: Sewn on uniforms to identify the players for fans by the University of Pittsburgh for a 1908 game against Washington & Jefferson. Without numbers, W&J won, 14-0.

1st radio broadcast: Long before any professional game was put on the air, a game between Texas U and Texas A&M was broadcast in November, 1920. An experimental radio station, WTAW, handled the play-by-play.

1st national broadcast: It originated in 1922 from Stagg Field, Chicago, and was a coast-to-coast description of a clash between the Princeton Tigers and Chicago University Maroons. WEAF of New York City relayed the broadcast nationally.

1st televised game: From Randall's Island, New York, came Fordham U's 34-7 win over Waynesburg College—TV'd on September 30, 1939. It was described as causing "a very minor sensation."

1st network color telecast: California Bears' 35-0 blanking of Penn U in 1951.

1st Bowl game telecast: Michigan's close 14-6 victory over California in the Rose Bowl game of 1951. A delayed telecast, it was seen in the East 2 days later by kinescope.

When a player's name appears in the NFL Manual of Records several times, he ranks with the greatest stars of the past 60 years. Only a handful of men have set all-time records in 5 or more categories.

At the very top are the *peerless ones*—players who established six or more marks which stand today as the best in history. The most prolific performers of all are:

1. **Jim Brown**
2. **George Blanda**
3. **O.J. Simpson**
4. **Sam Baugh**
5. **Fran Tarkenton**

Although these 5 superstars have been retired for an average of **15.3** seasons, their feats remain stupendous and unmatched. As Chicago Bears founder George Halas put it, "They were awesome." Their records:

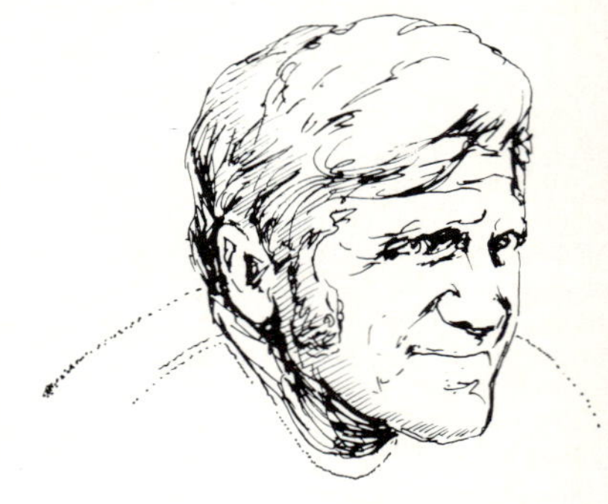

1 **James Nathaniel (Jim) Brown**, RB, 6′2″, 230 pounds (1957-1965)

Most yards gained rushing, career: 12,312

Most seasons leading league, rushing: 8

Highest average gain, rushing, career: 5.22 yards

Most consecutive years leading league, rushing: 5

Most touchdowns, career: 126 (106-r, 20-p)

Most games 100-or-more yards, rushing, career: 58

Most combined net yards gained, career (rushing, receiving, punt returns, interception returns, fumble returns): 15,459 yards

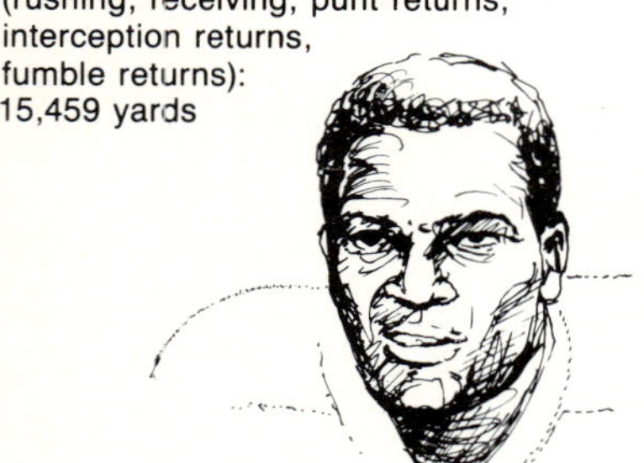

The foremost ground-gainer who ever lived, this ex-Syracuse U All-American fullback posted many of the rushing records in only 9 seasons with the Cleveland Browns (1957-65). He retired early, at age 29, to become a motion-picture actor. Traveling for more than 8¾ miles as a pro ball-packer (combined yards-rushes, receptions, etc.) he bowled over tacklers with power and a hammering forearm, plus speed and craftiness. From the **T**-formation, Brown could drive inside or outside, or catch passes with equal effectiveness. Despite broken bones, he never missed a game because of injury. Although in his day only 12 to 14 games were played per season, *Cannonball Jim* set another mark which still holds: rushing for more than 1,000 yards in 7 seasons.

Below huge shoulders, he tapered to a 31-inch waist. Brown spent his whole career with the Cleveland Browns, named not for him, but for Coach Paul Brown. He won the Jim Thorpe-Most Valuable Player of the NFL award 3 times, was elected to Pro Hall of Fame in 1971, and on his biggest touchdown day, made 5 TDs, all by rushing.

2 **George Frederick Blanda**, QB-K, 6′2″, 215 pounds (1949-1975)

Most seasons played: 26

Most games played, career: 340

Most points scored, career: 2,002

Most touchdown passes thrown, season: 36

Most field goals, career: 335

Most points-after-touchdown, season: 65

Most points-after-touchdown, career: 959

The most durable of all pros, *Old Folks* Blanda lasted from '49 through '75 and retired at age 48. With Chicago, Baltimore, Houston and Oakland, he was an unsurpassed quarterback-placekicker. Scoring more points than anyone in the game's annals, Blanda shares the all-time mark of 7 TD passes in one game, and once completed 37 passes in one game. He ran up 1,005 lifetime points on field goals with his magic toe. His total 2,002 points scored are 563 ahead of the nearest contender. Blanda was affectionately known as *the Terror of the Huddle* for chewing out teammates.

In a phenomenal streak at age 44, the burly blond won 6 straight games for Oakland with last-ditch TD passes and FGs. "I could play another 5 years if they'd only let me," complained George when they finally retired him. Blanda won NFL Most Valuable Player Award 1970, and called *The Timeless Wonder* , he was voted into the Pro Hall of Fame in 1981.

3 **Orenthal James *O.J.* Simpson**, RB, 6′1″, 212 pounds (1969-1979)

Most yards gained, rushing, season: 2,003

Most touchdowns, season: 23

Most games 200 or more yards, rushing, career: 6

Most consecutive games 100 yards, rushing: 7

Most games 100 or more yards, rushing: 11 (tied)

Most yards gained, rushing, career: 11,236

In 11 campaigns with the Buffalo Bills and San Francisco 49ers, *The Juice* did everything with the football but put it into orbit. A phantom break away back in college (USC), he won the Heisman Trophy in 1968, and was named College Player of the Decade for the '70s. A 9.4 sprinter, O.J. ran on a world record-setting USC relay team.

As a pro, he raced for more yardage than anyone except Jim Brown. The Buffalo Bills gave him sub-par blocking, yet he compiled more 100-yard-plus games in one season (11 in 1973) than any running back. At his best in an open field, Simpson once ran wild for 303 combined yards in one game.

Handsome O.J. went 94 yards for one of the NFL's longest TDs. (An O.J. oddity: His head was so large that a special helmet had to be constructed). Retiring to win prominence in Hollywood films, he's also famed for his hurdling-flying TV commercials. Simpson was voted the NFL's Most Valuable Player in 1973.

---

4 Samuel Adrian Baugh, QB-K, 6′2″, 180 pounds (1937-1952)

Most years leading league, passing: 6

Highest pass-completion percentage, season: 70.33

Highest average gain passing, game: 18.53 yards

Most seasons leading league, punting: 4

Highest average, punting, season: 51.4 yards

Highest average, punting, career: 45.10 yards

In 1937, the Washington Redskins introduced a tall, stringbean Texan in a 10-gallon hat and cowboy boots to the public. Fans loved him. Drawled *Slinging Sammy* Baugh, "After rasslin' steers down home, these football monsters don't bother me."

Baugh introduced a new passing style—the side-arm *slingshot.* His sharp bullet passes scattered defenses, changing the game from a rush-and-defend affair to an aerial circus. As a rookie, Baugh led the NFL in completions. And he continued to do so longer than any QB in history. Behind him, the Redskins won 7 Eastern Division titles and 2 World Championships. When Baugh and the Skins beat the Chicago Bears for the 1942 NFL crown, Sammy's share was $965 (compared to today's $18,000 winners' shares). The Texan was one of the first to throw for 400 yards in a single game, and no QB could kick like Sammy (who booted them as much as 90 yards and 30 years later still holds the mark for career average on kicks). Baugh lasted a remarkable 16 seasons and was named to the Hall of Fame in 1963.

Slinging Sammy Baugh (asked in 1935 to hit a pass-receiver in the eye): *"Which eye do you want me to hit?"*

---

5 Francis Asbury (Fran) Tarkenton, QB 6′, 185 pounds (1961-1978)

Most passes attempted, career: 6,467

Most passes completed, career: 3,686

Most yards gained passing, career: 47,003

Most touchdown passes, career: 342

Most season played with 3,000 or more completions: 18

Most Super Bowl completed passes, game: 18 (tied)

They called him *Fran the Scram*, the not-very-big field general who could wiggle out of anything. A *secret elixir* kept him going for 18 campaigns. In a 1977 game, Tarkenton's typical, madcap, all-over-the-field scramble lasted 28 seconds—and still he threw for a touchdown. "I call my own plays, not the coaches," boasted Fran, and it was true. Never seriously hurt despite his slight size, he was a confirmed gambler who'd pass from his own end zone at will. Probably no QB thrilled more fans with his daring and dodging. *The Scram* was criticized for passing 500 or more times a season, but his lifetime NFL record of 3,686 completions and 342 touchdowns is unequaled, effectively silencing critics. Fran also recovered more fumbles than any player in the 60 years of the NFL (43). Before retiring at age 38, he set another possible record—for "most TV appearances and commercials." Today, he's a popular TV series co-host.

Double Champion: Super athlete **Tom Brown** played outfield and first base for Washington in the 1963 *World Series.* Four years later he was in the *Super Bowl* as a defensive back for the Green Bay Packers.

But their hearts were whole... Born with a birth defect which gave him only half of one foot and no right hand, **Tom Dempsey** set a world record with his 63-yard winning field goal as the Saints beat the Detroit Lions in 1970. **Raymond Berry**, leading NFL receiver for 3 years, could barely see without glasses and suffered from tremedous pain due to back problems caused by a shorter leg.

Professional Football Records

The Most in a Career

Points:	2,002—George Blanda, Chicago Bears, 1949, 1950-58; Baltimore, 1950; Houston, 1960-66; Oakland, 1967-75 (9 TDs, 943 PATs, 335 FGs)
Touchdowns:	126—Jim Brown, Cleveland, 1957-65 (106-R, 20-P)
	113—Lenny Moore, Baltimore, 1956-67 (63-R, 48-P, 2-RET)
	105—Don Hutson, Green Bay, 1935-45 (3-R, 99-R, 3-RET)
Points After Touchdown:	943—George Blanda, Chicago Bears, 1949, 1950-58; Baltimore, 1950; Houston, 1960-66; Oakland, 1967-75
Consecutive Points After Touchdown:	234—Tommy Davis, San Francisco, 1959-65
Points After Touchdown, Percentage (200 PATs):	99.43—Tommy Davis, San Francisco, 1959-69 (350-348)
Yards Gained Rushing:	12,312—Jim Brown, Cleveland, 1957-65
Games, 100 or More Yards Rushing:	58—Jim Brown, Cleveland, 1957-65
Attempts Rushing:	2,462—Franco Harris, Pittsburgh, 1972-80
	2,404—O.J. Simpson, Buffalo, 1969-77; San Francisco, 1978-79
	2,359—Jim Brown, Cleveland, 1957-65
Yards Gained Rushing, Average (700 attempts):	5.22—Jim Brown, Cleveland, 1957-65 (2,359-12,312)
	5.14—Eugene *Mercury* Morris, Miami, 1969-75; San Diego, 1976 (804-4,133)
	5.00—Gale Sayers, Chicago, 1965-71 (991-4,956)
Yards Gained Passing:	47,003—Fran Tarkenton, Minnesota, 1961-66, 1972-78; N.Y. Giants, 1967-71
	40,239—Johnny Unitas, Baltimore, 1956-72; San Diego, 1973
	33,503—John Hadl, San Diego, 1962-72; Los Angeles, 1973-74; Green Bay, 1974-75; Houston, 1976-77
Passes Completed:	3,686—Fran Tarkenton, Minnesota, 1961-66, 1972-78; N.Y. Giants, 1967-71
	2,830—Johnny Unitas, Baltimore, 1956-72; San Diego, 1973
	2,469—John Brodie, San Francisco, 1957-73
Pass Completions, Percentage (1,500 attempts):	60.55—Ken Stabler, Oakland, 1970-79; Houston, 1980 (2,938-1,779)
	57.42—Bart Starr, Green Bay, 1956-71 (3,149-1,808)
	57.40—Dan Fouts, San Diego, 1973-80 (2,594-1,489)
Seasons Leading League, Passing:	6—Sammy Baugh, Washington, 1937, 1940, 1943, 1945, 1947, 1949
Seasons, 3,000 or More Yards Passing:	5—Sonny Jurgensen, Philadelphia, 1961-62; Washington, 1966-67, 1969
Yards Gained, Pass Receptions:	11,834—Don Maynard, N.Y. Giants, 1958; N.Y. Jets, 1960-72; St. Louis, 1973
	10,266—Lance Alworth San Diego, 1962-70; Dallas, 1971-72
	9,577—Harold Jackson, Los Angeles, 1968, 1973-77; Philadelphia, 1969-72; New England, 1978-80
Pass Receptions:	649—Charley Taylor, Washington, 1964-75, 1977
	633—Don Maynard, N.Y. Giants, 1958; N.Y. Jets, 1960-72; St. Louis, 1973
	631—Raymond Berry, Baltimore, 1955-67
Consecutive Games, Pass Receptions:	127—Harold Carmichael, Philadelphia, 1972-80
Seasons Leading League, Pass Receptions:	8—Don Hutson, Green Bay, 1936-37, 1939, 1941-45
Interceptions By:	81—Paul Krause, Washington, 1964-67; Minnesota, 1968-79
Yards Gained, Interceptions:	1,282—Emlen Tunnell, N.Y. Giants, 1948-58; Green Bay, 1959-61
	1,207—Dick *Night Train* Lane, Los Angeles, 1952-53; Chicago Cardinals, 1954-59; Detroit, 1960-65
	1,185—Paul Krause, Washington, 1964-67; Minnesota, 1968-69
Combined Net Yards Gained:	15,459—Jim Brown, Cleveland, 1957-65
	14,368—O.J. Simpson, Buffalo, 1969-77; San Francisco, 1978-79
	14,078—Bobby Mitchell, Cleveland, 1958-61; Washington, 1962-68
Yards Gained, Kickoff Returns:	6,922—Ron Smith, Chicago, 1965, 1970-72; Atlanta, 1966-67; Los Angeles, 1968-69; San Diego, 1973; Oakland, 1974
Highest Average Yards, Kickoff Returns (75 returns):	30.56—Gale Sayers, Chicago, 1965-71
Highest Average Yards, Punting (300 punts):	45.10—Sammy Baugh, Washington, 1937-52
Punts:	1,072—Jerrel Wilson, Kansas City, 1963-77; New England, 1978
Field Goals:	335—George Blanda, Chicago Bears, 1949, 1950-58; Baltimore, 1950; Houston, 1960-66; Oakland, 1967-75
Fumbles:	105—Roman Gabriel, Los Angeles, 1962-72; Philadelphia, 1973-77
Fumbles Recovered, Own and Opponents':	43—Fran Tarkenton, Minnesota, 1961-66, 1972-78; N.Y. Giants, 1967-71 (43 own)

The Most in a Season

Points:	176—Paul Hornung, Green Bay, 1960 (15 TDs, 41 PATs, 15 FGs)
Touchdowns:	23—O.J. Simpson, Buffalo, 1975 (16-r, 7-p)
Points After Touchdown:	64—George Blanda, Houston, 1961
Points After Touchdown, No Misses:	56—Danny Villanueva, Dallas, 1966
Yards Gained Rushing:	2,003—O.J. Simpson, Buffalo, 1973
Attempts Rushing:	373—Earl Campbell, Houston, 1980
	369—Walter Payton, Chicago, 1979
	368—Earl Campbell, Houston, 1979
Yards Gained Passing:	4,802—Dan Fouts, San Diego, 1981
Passes Completed:	360—Dan Fouts, San Diego, 1980
	347—Steve DeBerg, San Francisco, 1979
	345—Fran Tarkenton, Minnesota, 1978
Consecutive Passes Attempted, None Intercepted:	294—Bart Starr, Green Bay, 1964-65
	208—Milt Plum, Cleveland, 1959-60
	206—Roman Gabriel, Los Angeles, 1968-69

Interceptions By:	14—Dick *Night Train* Lane, Los Angeles, 1952
Combined Net Yards Gained:	2,462—Terry Metcalf, St. Louis, 1975 2,444—Mack Herron, New England, 1974 2,440—Gale Sayers, Chicago, 1966
Field Goals:	34—Jim Turner, N.Y. Jets, 1968
Consecutive Field Goals:	20—Garo Yepremiam, Miami, 1978; New Orleans, 1979
Fumbles:	17—Dan Pastorini, Houston, 1973
Rookie, Points:	132—Gale Sayers, Chicago, 1965 (22 TDs)
Rookie, Touchdowns:	22—Gale Sayers, Chicago, 1965 (14-R, 6-P, 2-RET)

The Most in a Game

Points:	40—Ernie Nevers, Chicago Cardinals vs. Chicago Bears, 1929 (6 TDs, 4 PATs)
Yards Gained Rushing:	275—Walter Payton, Chicago vs. Minnesota, 1977 273—O.J. Simpson, Buffalo vs. Detroit, 1976 250—O.J. Simpson, Buffalo vs. New England, 1973
Attempts Rushing:	41—Franco Harris, Pittsburgh vs. Cincinnati, 1976 40—Lydell Mitchell, Baltimore vs. N.Y. Jets, 1974 40—Walter Payton, Chicago vs. Minnesota, 1977
Yards Gained Passing:	554—Norm Van Brocklin, Los Angeles vs. N.Y. Yanks, 1951 505—Y.A. Tittle, N.Y. Giants vs. Washington, 1962 496—Joe Namath, N.Y. Jets vs. Baltimore, 1972
Passes Completed:	42—Richard Todd, N.Y. Jets vs. San Francisco, 1980 38—Tommy Kramer, Minnesota vs. Cleveland, 1980 37—George Blanda, Houston vs. Buffalo, 1964
Yards Gained, Pass Receptions:	303—Jim Benton, Cleveland vs. Detroit, 1945 302—Cloyce Box, Detroit vs. Baltimore, 1950 272—Charley Hennigan, Houston vs. Boston, 1961
Combined Net Yards Gained:	373—Billy Cannon, Houston vs. N.Y. Titans, 1961 341—Timmy Brown, Philadelphia vs. St. Louis, 1962 339—Gale Sayers, Chicago vs. Minnesota, 1966
Yards Gained, Kickoff Returns:	294—Wally Triplett, Detroit vs. Los Angeles, 1950
Highest Average Yards, Punting (4 punts):	61.75—Bob Cifers, Detroit vs. Chicago Bears, 1946
Field Goals:	7—Jim Bakken, St. Louis vs. Pittsburgh, 1967
Fumbles:	7—Len Dawson, Kansas City vs. San Diego, 1964

The Longest in a Game

Run From Scrimmage:	97—Andy Uram, Green Bay vs. Chicago Cardinals, 1939 97—Bob Gage, Pittsburgh vs. Chicago Bears, 1949
Pass Completion:	99—Frank Filchock (to Farkas), Washington vs. Pittsburgh, 1939 99—George Izo (to Mitchell), Washington vs. Cleveland, 1963 99—Karl Sweetan (to Studstill), Detroit vs. Baltimore, 1966 99—Sonny Jurgensen (to Allen), Washington vs. Chicago, 1968
Interception Return:	102—Bob Smith, Detroit vs. Chicago Bears, 1949 102—Erich Barnes, N.Y. Giants vs. Dallas Cowboys, 1962 102—Gary Barbaro, Kansas City vs. Seattle, 1977 101—Richie Petitbon, Chicago vs. Los Angeles, 1962 101—Henry Carr, N.Y. Giants vs. Los Angeles, 1966 101—Tony Greene, Buffalo vs. Kansas City, 1976
Kickoff Return:	106—Al Carmichael, Green Bay vs. Chicago Bears, 1956 106—Noland Smith, Kansas City vs. Denver, 1967 106—Roy Green, St. Louis vs. Dallas, 1979
Punt:	98—Steve O'Neal, N.Y. Jets vs. Denver, 1969 94—Joe Lintzenich, Chicago Bears vs. N.Y. Giants, 1931 90—Don Chandler, Green Bay vs. San Francisco, 1965
Field Goal:	63—Tom Dempsey, New Orleans vs. Detroit, 1970
Return of Missed Field Goal:	101—Al Nelson, Philadelphia vs. Dallas, 1971
Fumble Run:	104—Jack Tatum, Oakland vs. Green Bay, 1972 (Opp)

The Most By a Team

Points, Game:	72—Washington vs. N.Y. Giants, 1966
Points, Both Teams, Game:	113—Washington (72) vs. N.Y. Giants (41), 1966
Points, Season:	513— Houston, 1961
Games Won, One Season (includes post-season games):	17—Miami, 1972 17—Pittsburgh, 1978
Consecutive	
Games Won (Regular Season):	17—Chicago Bears, 1933-34
Games Won, One Season (includes post-season games):	18—Chicago Bears, 1933-34, 1941-42 18—Miami, 1972-73
Home Games Won:	26—Miami, 1971-74
Home Games Without Defeat:	30—Green Bay, 1928-33 (won 27, tied 3)
Road Games Without Defeat:	13—Chicago Bears, 1941-43 (won 12, tied 1)
Games Lost:	26—Tampa Bay, 1976-77
Seasons Leading League:	9—Chicago Bears, 1934-35, 1939, 1941-43, 1946-47, 1956
Seasons League Champion:	11—Green Bay, 1929-31, 1936, 1939, 1944, 1961-62, 1965-67
***Fewest* Points, Season (since 1932):**	37—Cincinnati/St. Louis, 1934

The Most...

Seasons Played:	26—George Blanda, Chicago Bears, 1949, 1950-58; Baltimore, 1950; Houston, 1960-66; Oakland, 1967-75
Games Played:	340—George Blanda, Chicago Bears, 1949, 1950-58; Baltimore, 1950; Houston, 1960-66; Oakland, 1967-75
Consecutive Games Played:	282—Jim Marshall, Cleveland, 1960; Minnesota, 1961-79
Seasons As Coach:	40—George Halas, Chicago Bears, 1920-29, 1933-42, 1946-55, 1958-67

The Day It Rained Touchdowns: One hundred and thirteen points in a single game...the greatest scoring orgy in NFL history!

It happened November 27, 1966. In 3 hours, the Washington Redskins and New York Giants gave 50,439 fans more wild action than was ever dished up.
The menu included:

- Touchdown sprints of 45, 62 and 50 yards
- A 74-yard touchdown pass play
- A 52-yard touchdown return of a punt
- A 62-yard touchdown run from an interception
- A total of 14 extra points kicked
- 49 passes and 30 completions
- A 16 touchdown total
- 5 touchdowns scored in 6 min., 17 secs.

The game wasn't close—Washington won it, 72-41—but it still stands as the most explosive single contest in the many decades of pro football.

Wildest Few Seconds: "An absolute impossibility happened today at Forbes Field," wrote a Pittsburgh sports scribe on one October day in 1945. In the space of ***35 seconds***, the New York Giants, behind **Arnie Herber's** passing, ran up 3 touchdowns and 21 points to win a game. And that's still the NFL high for most points tallied in so little time.

One-Man Gang Syndrome: Hall of Famer **Ernie Nevers** started it in 1929 when he powered his way to 6 touchdowns in one day for the St. Louis Cardinals—the first time that had happened.

Twenty-two years later, **Dub Jones** of Cleveland equaled Nevers' feat with touchdown runs of 2, 34, 27, 43, 43 and 62 yards against the Chicago Bears. Some experts thought they'd never see such a sight again.

Then came a Chicago Bears-San Francisco 49ers game in 1965, and a flashy rookie running back for the Bears named **Gale Sayers.** On a muddy field, Sayers scored from 80, 21, 7, 51 and 1 yards out. In the waning moments of the fourth period, he caught a punt and went 75 yards—to join **Nevers** and **Jones** in that magic circle consisting of the only backs ever to score a sextet of TDs in a single contest.

Record Goofs: Department of Utter Futility

Some of the finest players have chalked up all-time worst performances, proving the maxim: "Both heroes and bums put their pants on the same way—one leg at a time."

Most fumbles, career:
1. **Roman Gabriel**, Los Angeles: 105
2. **Johnny Unitas**, Baltimore: 95

Most fumbles, season:
1. **Dan Pastorini**, Houston: 17
2. **Don Meredith**, Dallas; **Joe Cribbs**, Buffalo; **Steve Fuller**, Kansas City: 16

Most fumbles, game:
1. **Len Dawson**, Kansas City: 7
2. **Sam Etcheverry**, St. Louis: 6

Most passes had intercepted, game:
1. **Jim Hardy**, St. Louis Cardinals: 8
2. Held by various passers: 7

Longest wrong-way run:
Jim Marshall's historic 1964 gallop in the wrong direction. The Minnesota end scooped up a loose-ball fumble and ran 66 yards into his own end zone, giving San Francisco a safety. (But The Vikings won despite the blunder, 27-22).

Worst team performance, won-lost:
1. The Detroit Lions of 1942 lost every game, scored only 38 points the entire season and were shut out 5 times.
2. The Dallas Texans of 1952 were another disaster, winners of but a single game all season.
3. The Dallas Cowboys weren't always mighty. In the first season of their organization (1960), they won none, lost 11 games and tied 1.
4. In recent years, the champion *Sad Sacks* were the Chicago Bears of 1979: won 1, lost 13.

Most consecutive games lost:
1. Tampa Bay: 26
2. Chicago Cardinals: 19
3. Oakland Raiders: 19

Fewest yards gained rushing, game:
1. Detroit vs. Chicago Cardinals: minus 53 yards
2. Philadelphia vs. Chicago Bears: minus 36 yards
3. Pittsburgh vs. Brooklyn: minus 33 yards

Fewest yards gained passing, game:
1. Denver vs. Oakland: minus 53 yards
2. Cincinnati vs. Houston: minus 52 yards
3. Atlanta vs. San Francisco: minus 39 yards

Field goals: On a windy day in Pittsburgh on September 24, 1967, **Jim Bakken** of the St. Louis Cardinals set a prodigious field goal record—kicking 7 through the uprights. Despite a twisting wind, the *Wisconsin Howitzer* booted FG's of 18, 24, 33, 29, 24, 32 and 23 yards.

Behind Bakken rank: Garo Yepremiam, Jim Turner, Tom Dempsey and **Bobby Howfield** with 6 FGs in one afternoon.

Department of Long Returns: Perhaps the rarest, most spectacular sight in pro football is the 100-yard-or-more gain on the return of a punt, kickoff, interception or fumble recovery.

Longest punt return for touchdown:
1. **Gil LeFebvre**, Cincinnati; **Charlie West, Minnesota; Dennis Morgan**, Dallas: 98 yards
2. ***Bullet Bill* Dudley**, Washington: 96 yards

Longest kickoff return with touchdown:
1. **Al Carmichael**, Green Bay; **Noland Smith,** Kansas City; **Roy Green**, St. Louis: 106 yards
2. Held by various players: 105 yards

Longest pass-interception run for a touchdown:
1. **Bob Smith,** Detroit; **Erich Barnes,** N.Y. Giants; **Gary Barbaro,** Kansas City; **Louis Breeden,** Cincinnati: 102 yards
2. Held by various players: 101 yards

Longest fumble return for a touchdown:
1. **Jack Tatum**, Oakland: 104 yards
2. **George Halas**, Chicago Bears: 96
3. **Chuck Howley**, Dallas: 97

In 1960, Dallas quarterback **Eddie LaBaron** threw a 2-inch pass to Dick Bielski—the shortest pass on record. It was a touchdown pass.

Average Punt: 37 yards
Average Punt Return: 9 yards
Average Run gain: 3 yards
Average Completed Pass gain: 7 yards

Sample Itinerary: Rams vs. Saints

Saturday, Sept. 12

8:00AM	*Report to Los Angeles Airport*
9:00AM	*Depart via United Airlines*
2:33PM	*Arrive in New Orleans. Buses leave immediately for Dome Stadium to dress for practice. Practice site to be announced. After practice, leave for hotel*
9:00PM	*Special team meeting*
9:30PM	*Team Meeting: Offense in Melrose Room; Defense in Rosedown Room*
10:00PM	*Hamburger buffet*
11:00PM	*Curfew!*

Sunday, Sept. 13

7:00AM	*Wake-up call*
7:30AM	*Religious Services*
8:00AM	*Pre-game meal*
9:45AM	*Bus 1 departs for Stadium*
10:00AM	*Bus 2 departs for Stadium*
10:10AM	*Bus 3 departs for Stadium (media)*
11:00AM	*Early birds on the field*
11:15AM	*Entire squad on the field*
12:00 Noon	**Kickoff—Rams vs. New Orleans Saints**
5:00PM	*Depart via United Airlines*
6:55PM	*Arrive at Los Angeles Airport*

Monday, Sept. 14

9:00AM	*Bumps and bruises*
12:30PM	*Special team meeting*
1:00PM	*Team meeting 2 mile run*

Nicknames

Nicknames have colorfully decorated the game from its beginning. Nobody knows who was first to be given a monicker, but it might have been *Samson* (real name Lawson) Fiscus, one of the first college men to turn pro in the 1890s.

Among the most famous nicknames (proper name listed) have been:

1920s-1930s:
Hunk Anderson (Heartley)
Curly Lambeau (Earl)
Turk Edwards (Albert)
Buckets Goldenberg (Charles)
Tuffy Leemans (Alphonse)
Total name change: Johnny Blood (John McNally)

1940s:
Bulldog Turner (Clyde)
Bullet Bill Dudley (William)
Whizzer White (Byron)
Bucko Kilroy (Frank)
Antelope Hutson (Don)

1950s:
Bruiser Kinard (Frank)
Crazy Legs Hirsch (Elroy)
The Geek (Bob St.Clair)
Tank Younger (Paul)
Night Train Lane (Dick)
Vitamin T. Smith (Verda)

1960s:
Deacon Jones (David)
Mercury Morris (Eugene)
Bambi Alworth (Lance)
Dandy Don Meredith
Broadway Joe Namath
Killer Karras (Alex)

1970s:
Dr. Doom (Dave Wilcox)
Tommy *The Thing* Nobis
O.J. *Juice* Simpson (Orenthal)
Isiah *Black Panther* Robertson
Thor Siemon (Jeff)
Rocky Bleier (Robert)
Buck Buchanan (Junious)
Fran The Scram Tarkenton (Francis)

1980s:
Snake Stabler (Ken)
Hacksaw Reynolds (Jack)
Stork Hendricks (Ted)
Billy *White Shoes* Johnson
Ron *Polish Rifle* Jaworski
Big Sky Montana (Joe)
Roger *The Dodger* Staubach

Team Names

Few fans know how pro teams got their names. For instance, the **Los Angeles *Rams***, before moving west in 1946, were the Cleveland Rams—a title picked by owner **Homer Marshman** in 1937. Marshman explained, "Wild rams butt heads harder than any animal." He also admired the Fordham University Rams.

Other name origins, courtesy of NFL historians:

Original owner **Barron Hilton** took the **San Diego *Chargers*** name from the battle cry of University of Southern California Students—"CHA-A-A-A-RGE!"

Since the **Detroit** baseball team was called the Tigers, football pioneers one-upped the horsehiders by becoming the king of beasts: ***Lions.***

Green Bay's *Packers* evolved from their early-day sponsorship by the Indian and Acme Packing Companies.

New Orleans adopted its heavenly nickname from one of part-owner **Al Hirt's** favorite trumpet numbers: *When The **Saints** Go Marching In.*

A lady named **Mrs. Robert Swanson** named **Miami** in a statewide contest, saying, "The dolphin is intelligent and indigenous to this area." This saved the ***Dolphins*** from becoming the Swordfish or Navel Oranges.

A Georgia lady schoolteacher, pointing out that the falcon is a "proud bird full of courage and fight", is credited with christening the **Atlanta *Falcons.***

Cleveland's *Browns* were named for their first coach and team architect, **Paul Brown**, when they began in 1948 as a member of the old All-America Conference. No other coach has had a team named for him.

Philadelphia *Eagles* owner **Bert Bell** adopted the eagle of President Franklin D. Roosevelt's National Recovery Act (NRA) in 1933. It was said that Bell had brought "a new deal, a new franchise" to the city.

Founder **Chris O'Brien** cut equipment costs by buying used, faded maroon jerseys from the University of Chicago Maroons for his new **Chicago** pro team, which he then could only name: the ***Cardinals.***

Houston is the ***Oilers*** simply because their owner, **Bud Adams**, was in the oil business. "You think I'd ever call them the Aluminums or Uraniums?" asked Adams.

Collegiate Bowl Games

In 1902 a simple flower pageant turned into the Rose Bowl game—touching off the wildest scramble in football annals.

Every college covets a Bowl bid, especially to one of the *Big Four:* Rose, Orange, Cotton and Sugar. As of 1981, television networks paid the Big Four from $2.5 to $5.2 million per game for broadcast rights. Schools reaching the major bowls collect as much as $200,000 plus expenses.

The 80-year old Rose Bowl, now seating 105,000, is the grandfather of all post-season classics. Next oldest are the Orange Bowl (Miami) and Sugar Bowl (New Orleans). Both began in 1935. In 1937 the Cotton Bowl (Dallas) made its debut. Each bowl sends out scouts in December, seeking to sign up the most promising teams well before the season is concluded.

Policy at the august Rose Bowl (a former Pasadena garbage dump located in a canyon called the Arroyo Seco) is to present only the respective champions of the Big Ten and Pacific Ten conferences. An exclusive deal was signed between the Rose Bowl and the 2 conferences in 1947. The Big Ten, led by Illinois and Michigan, won the first 6 games of the series. But the Pacific Ten rallied thereafter and is threatening to tie the all-time standings. At the conclusion of the 1982 contest, the score stood:

Big Ten—19 wins
Pacific Ten—17 wins

The heaviest winners: USC (9 games); Ohio State (5), Michigan (4), Washington (4).

Result of the first Rose Bowl (1902): Michigan 49, Stanford 0, a Western disaster.

Result of latest, 1982 game: Washington 28, Iowa 0, a rare shutout.

Most lopsided victories:
Illinois 45, UCLA 14 (1947)
Michigan 49, USC 0 (1948)
Illinois 40, Stanford 7 (1952)
Washington 44, Wisconsin 8 (1960)
USC 42, Ohio State 17 (1973)

Only game not played at the Rose Bowl: Played at Duke University, Durham, N.C., 1942, during a Pacific Coast wartime blackout.

COTTON BOWL

Texas goes wild when the U of Texas Longhorns are in the *Cotton*—and the Horns have been there 18 times in 45 games. Ten times they've won, 8 times they've brought statewide gloom by losing. Texas-Notre Dame is a great series here, with the Irish copping 2 of 3 matches. For some reason, the Cotton produces some of the closest battles anywhere in collegiana, as witness:

1970: Texas 21, Notre Dame 17
1973: Texas 17, Alabama 13
1979: Notre Dame 35, Houston 34
(one of the greatest Bowl games ever played)
1980: Houston 17, Nebraska 14
1982: Texas 14, Alabama 12

SUGAR BOWL

Most of the *financial* sugar from this Bowl has gone to Coach **Paul *Bear* Bryant's** Alabama Crimson Tide in recent seasons. The Tide clinched the national championship here in both 1978 and 1979, beating Ohio State and Penn State in brawls that rivaled even the Rose Bowl's television ratings. The Sugar Bowl is region-proud, favoring the use of southern teams—although the Air Force (from Colorado) and Pittsburgh have appeared.

ORANGE BOWL

The Miami classic, now in its 47th year, began modestly. In the 1930's it featured numerous small-time football schools, but came of age by attracting the biggies from 1942 onward. The Orange Bowl strives to land the nation's least-beaten team. Dominant colleges: Penn State, led by Coach **Joe Paterno**, won all the *Oranges* in 1969-70 and 1974; Nebraska won 3 straight games in 1971-72 and 1973; Oklahoma scored a straight *triple* in 1979-80 and 1981.

Greatest feat: Behind little (5'9") **Johnny Rodgers**, Nebraska's Cornhuskers beat Alabama, 38-6 and Notre Dame, 40-6 in consecutive Orange Bowls, 1972-73.

OTHER BOWLS

Gone from the frenzied post season picture (a good thing, say some critics) are such Bowls as the Raisin, Grape, Oil, Alamo, Mercy, Delta, Bacardi, Aviation and Gotham. Currently in action and regionally important are:
Sun Bowl (El Paso, Texas)
Gator Bowl (Jacksonville, Florida)
Bluebonnet Bowl (Houston, Texas)
Tangerine Bowl (Orlando, Florida)
Liberty Bowl (Memphis, Tennessee)
Peach Bowl (Atlanta, Georgia)
Fiesta Bowl (Tempe, Arizona)
Independence Bowl (Shreveport, Louisiana)
Holiday Bowl (San Diego, California)
Hall of Fame Classic (Birmingham, Alabama)
Aloha Bowl (Honolulu, Hawaii)

Biggest Bowl gadabout: Alabama U's team was once known as the *Red Elephants* and has lived up to the name by being a traveling circus—35 Bowl appearances in school history (won 19, lost 13, tied 3). Next most Bowl-happy is Texas U with 28 Bowl appearances, followed by USC and Georgia with 25 each and Oklahoma and Louisiana State with 22 each. *America's Team*—Notre Dame—has, oddly, appeared only 10 times, winning 7.

Worst Bowl record: Iowa State and Utah State with 4 defeats in 4 appearances each.

Dutch Meyer, Texas Christian Coach, 1933 (in halftime speech): *"Men, yu've got 30 minutes to play and a lifetime to think about what happened."*

Tommy Lewis, Alabama U player (after he left his seat on the bench, ran onto the field and tackled touchdown-bound Rice player Dickie Moegle): *"I guess I'm just too full of Alabama."*

Super Bowl XVI

Coach **Bill Walsh's** gimmick plays and Quarterback **Joe Montana's** mixed-bag play-calling gave the San Francisco **49ers** a spectacular 26-21 win over Cincinnati. Losing quarterback **Ken Anderson** set a Super Bowl mark of 25 pass completions. But 49er wile and goal-line stands triumphed. **Montana** was named Most Valuable Player. Another record: $18,000 to each 49er for his efforts.

Super Bowl XV

The silver-and-black **Raiders** posted a second Super Bowl win by walloping the Eagles. The game featured TD bombs fired by QB **Jim Plunkett** to **Cliff Branch** and **Kenny King**, including a Super-record 80-yard pass-run.

Super Bowl XIV

LA's Rams, after a mediocre season, surprised everyone by reaching the Great Game—but succumbed after a battle to the Pittsburgh **Steelers.** QB **Terry Bradshaw**, the *Bald Eagle*, was the MVP and the Steelers scored their 4th Super victory.

Super Bowl XIII

One of the all-time fine pass-snarers, **John Stallworth** of the **Steelers** had a lot to do with Pittsburgh's hairbreadth win over Miami. ***Big John*** caught 2 TD passes in one of the tightest championship games ever played.

Super Bowl XII

Dallas **Cowboys'** power and *IQ* (interception quotient) ruled the day over upstart Denver. QB **Craig Morton** of the losers was intercepted a record 4 times under relentless pressure. Cowboy QB, **Roger Staubach** was, as always, sharper than a serpent's tooth.

Super Bowl XI

The Oakland **Raiders** piled up 429 yards on offense behind the running of **Clarence Davis** and coasted to an easy win. One of the duller Super Bowls, Minnesota lost in this classic for the 4th time.

Super Bowl X

Two titans clashed—and the Eastern powerhouse, Pittsburgh, won a squeaker. It was a second straight Super win for the **Steelers**, with MVP **Lynn Swann** starring on the receiving end of **Terry Bradshaw** bullets.

Super Bowl IX

A forgettable title match, the hallftime score was 2-0 and things didn't improve much in a lacklustre **Steelers'** march over the Vikings. **Franco Harris**, the MVP, was splendid for the winners as fullback.

Super Bowl VIII

One of the easiest wins a Super team ever registered. It was Miami's **Dolphins** all the way behind the combo of *Crusher* **Larry Csonka** (MVP) and ***Killer Jim*** **Klick.** The Vikings looked bad.

Super Bowl VII

The defeated Redskins scored just once—but it was an epic TD when Miami's placekicker **Garo Yepremiam** tried to turn passer after a fouled-up field-goal try. **Mike Bass** intercepted **Garo** for a TD that gave the **Dolphins** a headstart. Miami's dandy safety, **Jake Scott**, was MVP.

Super Bowl VI

Critics who swore the Dallas mob couldn't win the Big One were silenced (and the bookmakers wept) when the **Cowboys** absolutely clobbered Miami. MVP was **Roger** ***The Dodger*** **Staubach** of Dallas.

Super Bowl V

Compounding one error after another, the Baltimore **Colts** and Dallas Cowboys performed like zombies in the *Blooper* Bowl. 6 passes were intercepted, and there were fumbles galore. MVP honors went to Cowboy linebacker **Chuck Howley.**

Super Bowl IV

A pre-game gambling probe involving Kansas City QB **Len Dawson** highlighted a prosaic victory by the **Chiefs.** The exonerated **Dawson** was red hot with his passes and KC's defense shut down Minnesota rushing to a mere 67 yards. Guess who the MVP was—the abused Dawson.

Super Bowl III

Broadway Joe **Namath** predicted, "We'll beat them"—and to the shock of the Baltimore Colts he and the **Jets** did just that. This gave the bookies their worst of all beatings. **Jim Turner** kicked 3 FGs for the Jets and the injured **Johnny Unitas** wasn't enough to save the day for the Colts. A hysterically happy *Broadway* Joe was named MVP.

Super Bowl II

In **Vince Lombardi's** final game as Green Bay coach, the ***Pack*** ran over Oakland by a 19-point margin. MVP **Bart Starr** passed the ball and directed the win; **Don** ***Automatic*** **Chandler** booted 4 FGs for the victors.

Super Bowl I

In the initial Super Bowl, the whole United States came to a standstill to watch the Green Bay **Packers** build on a slim 14-10 halftime lead and put down the surprisingly tough Kansas City Chiefs. The hero was reserve end **Max McGree**, who caught 2 TD passes, along with **Elijah Pitts**, who ran for 2 TDs. QB **Bart Starr** was an easy MVP pick.

Franco Harris

Super Bowl I, first of the world championship series in 1967, was a box office flop. Only 63,036 fans showed up at the giant Los Angeles Coliseum to watch Green Bay romp over the Kansas City Chiefs, 35-10. *Estimated gate receipts: $750,000.*

But the players were happy: The Packers received $15,000 each and the losers collected $7,500 each. That was the highest payoff for a single game up to that date.

Super Bowl II in 1968 caught on with a bang. Transferred to Miami's Orange Bowl, it drew 75,546 and TV money made it the first $3 million gate in pro history.

After that, the Super Bowl bounced around to various locations—7 arenas in all. The stagings:

1. Orange Bowl (5 times)
2. Tulane Stadium, New Orleans (3)
3. Rose Bowl, Louisiana Superdome, L.A. Coliseum (2 each)
4. Rice University Stadium, Pontiac Silverdome (1 each)

Who named it? Lamar Hunt, owner of the Kansas City Chiefs, is credited with suggesting *Super Bowl* in 1966.

Attendance: The record gate for 16 *Supers* held to date was set in 1980 at the Rose Bowl, Pasadena, for Super Bowl XIV—103,985. More than 1,130,000 paying customers have watched these 16 games. Tickets reportedly have been scalped for as high as $1,500.

Is a celebration connected with the Super Bowl? Before the 1982 contest at the Silverdome in Pontiac, Michigan, the NFL threw a party for 3,000 at which 4,500 canapes, 3,500 chicken breasts and several vats of liquor were consumed.

The *Ins* and the *Outs* (a sad story): Thirteen teams of 28 in the NFL, including such longtime standbys as the Chicago Bears, New York Giants and Cleveland Browns, have never appeared in a Super Bowl. Other non-qualifiers: Buffalo, New England, Houston, San Diego, Seattle, St. Louis, Detroit, Tampa Bay, Atlanta and New Orleans.

Of the 15 clubs that have appeared, the Pittsburgh Steelers are preeminent. Only 5 teams have 2 or more victories in the series. The standings:

1. Pittsburgh: won 4, lost 0
2. Green Bay: won 2, lost 0
3. Miami: won 2, lost 1
4. Oakland: won 2, lost 1
5. Dallas: won 2, lost 3

The Super Heroes: Crunching Steeler fullback **Franco Harris'** 24 career points and 4 touchdowns in the Super Bowl lead all rushers.

Roger Staubach (Dallas) completed the most Super Bowl passes (61). Steeler quarterback **Terry Bradshaw** has thrown the most touchdowns (9).

Pittsburgh receiver **Lynn Swann** snared more passes (16) for more yards (364) than any other.

1982 Super Bowl stats: CBS paid $6 million for TV rights to San Francisco's 26-21 win over the Cincinnati Bengals at the Silverdome. Spectators paid in $3.34 million. Gross receipts were upward of $10 million. Winning player shares set a record at $18,000; the losers got $9,000.

It's difficult to believe, but for 7 straight years, between 1973-1978, a quarterback **did not** win the *Most Valuable Player* trophy at the Super Bowl.

In the 16 *Supers* contested to date, the pass-tossers were the big heroes and won MVP honors 9 times. But during one long stretch, the hottest guy on the field was a linebacker, running back, wide receiver, defensive end or defensive tackle.

Only 2 quarterbacks—**Bart Starr** of the Green Bay Packers and **Terry Bradshaw** of the Pittsburgh Steelers—have won the MVP award twice. The **Dallas Cowboys** and **Steelers** are tied for most Super Bowl winners with 4 each.

The complete list:

Super Bowl MVPs by Year

Game	Player	Pos.	Team
1967 I	Bart Starr	QB	Green Bay
1968 II	Bart Starr	QB	Green Bay
1969 III	Joe Namath	QB	NY Jets
1970 IV	Len Dawson	QB	Kansas City
1971 V	Chuck Howley	LB	Dallas
1972 VI	Roger Staubach	QB	Dallas
1973 VII	Jake Scott	DB	Miami
1974 VIII	Larry Csonka	RB	Miami
1975 IX	Franco Harris	RB	Pittsburgh
1976 X	Lynn Swann	WR	Pittsburgh
1977 XI	Fred Biletnikoff	WR	Oakland
1978 XII	Harvey Martin	DE	Dallas
	Randy White	DT	Dallas
1979 XIII	Terry Bradshaw	QB	Pittsburgh
1980 XIV	Terry Bradshaw	QB	Pittsburgh
1981 XV	Jim Plunkett	QB	Oakland
1982 XVI	Joe Montana	QB	San Francisco

Super oddities: In 2 games—New York Jets vs. Baltimore in '69 and Miami vs. Minnesota in '74—not a touchdown was registered by passing.

Roger *The Dodger* Staubach, elusive Dallas passer, was *sacked* (tackled down) a record 7 times in 1976 by an angry Pittsburgh defense.

In 1973, Miami and the Washington Redskins struggled all afternoon and produced only 21 points together—a day of futility.

In Pittsburgh's wild 35-31 win over Dallas in '79, 42 of 66 total points came from passes (7 touchdown throws, both teams).

A nonstop tragedy: Making 4 Super Bowl appearances, the powerful Minnesota Vikings won none, giving up an overall 95 points to 34 scored.

Super Bowl Results

Game	Date	Winner	Loser	Site	Attendance
XVI	1-24-82	**San Francisco (NFC) 26**	Cincinnati (AFC) 21	Pontiac	80,638
XV	1-25-81	**Oakland (AFC) 27**	Philadelphia (NFC) 10	New Orleans	76,135
XIV	1-20-80	**Pittsburgh (AFC) 31**	Los Angeles (NFC) 19	Pasadena	103,985
XIII	1-21-79	**Pittsburgh (AFC) 35**	Dallas (NFC) 31	Miami	79,484
XII	1-15-28	**Dallas (NFC) 27**	Denver (AFC) 10	New Orleans	75,583
XI	1- 9-77	**Oakland (AFC) 32**	Minnesota (NFC) 14	Pasadena	103,438
X	1-18-76	**Pittsburgh (AFC) 21**	Dallas (NFC) 17	Miami	80,187
IX	1-12-75	**Pittsburgh (AFC) 16**	Minnesota (NFC) 6	New Orleans	80,997
VIII	1-13-74	**Miami (AFC) 24**	Minnesota (NFC) 7	Houston	71,882
VII	1-14-73	**Miami (AFC) 14**	Washington (NFC) 7	Los Angeles	90,182
VI	1-16-72	**Dallas (NFC) 24**	Miami (AFC) 3	New Orleans	81,023
V	1-17-71	**Baltimore (AFC) 16**	Dallas (NFC) 13	Miami	79,204
IV	1-11-70	**Kansas City (AFL) 23**	Minnesota (NFL) 7	New Orleans	80,562
III	1-12-69	**New York (AFL) 16**	Baltimore (NFL) 7	Miami	75,389
II	1-14-68	**Green Bay (NFL) 33**	Oakland (AFL) 14	Miami	75,546
I	1-15-67	**Green Bay (NFL) 35**	Kansas City (AFL) 10	Los Angeles	61,946

Records Set and Tied in Super Bowl XVI

Records Set:

Most Passes Completed, Game
25, Ken Anderson, Cincinnati (old record: 18, Fran Tarkenton VIII, Ron Jaworski XV)
Most Passes Completed, Game,
Both Teams 39, Cincinnati (25) vs. San Francisco (14) (old record: 36, Minnesota and Oakland XI)
Most Pass Receptions, Game
11, Dan Ross, Cincinnati
(old record: 8, George Sauer, III)
Most First Downs, Game, Team
24, Cincinnati vs. San Francisco
(old record: 23, Dallas vs. Miami VI)
Most First Downs, Game, Both Teams
44, Cincinnati (24) vs. San Francisco (20)
(old record: 41, Oakland and Minnesota XI)
Most First Downs by Penalty, Game, Both Teams
6, Cincinnati (4) vs. San Francisco (2)
(old record: 5, accomplished twice)
Longest Scoring Drive, Team
92 yards, San Francisco vs. Cincinnati
(old record: 89 yards, Dallas vs. Pittsburgh XIII)
Largest Halftime Lead, Team
20-0, San Francisco vs. Cincinnati
(oid record: 17-0, Miami vs. Minnesota VIII)
Highest Completion Percentage, Game, Team
73.5, 25-of-34, Cincinnati vs. San Francisco
(old record: 67.9, Dallas vs. Denver XII)

Records Tied:

Most Field Goals, Game, Team
4, San Francisco vs. Cincinnati
(tied Green Bay vs. Oakland II)
Most Touchdowns, Game
2, Dan Ross, Cincinnati,
(shared by eight other players)
Most Kickoff Returns, Game
5, David Verser, Cincinnati
(shared by two other players)
Most Points, Fourth Quarter, Team
14, Cincinnati vs. San Francisco
(shared by four other teams)
Most First Downs by Penalty, Game, Team
4, Cincinnati vs. San Francisco
(shared by two other teams)
Most Players, 100-or-more Yards on Pass Receptions, Game, Team
2, Cincinnati vs. San Francisco
(Collinsworth 107, Ross 104)
(tied Pittsburgh vs. Dallas XIII, Stallworth and Swann)
Most Kickoff Returns, Game, Team
7, Cincinnati vs. San Francisco
(shared by two other teams)

This is the first time in 16 Super Bowls that the team that gained the most yards from scrimmage lost the game. (Cincinnati outgained San Francisco, 356 yards to 275 yards.)

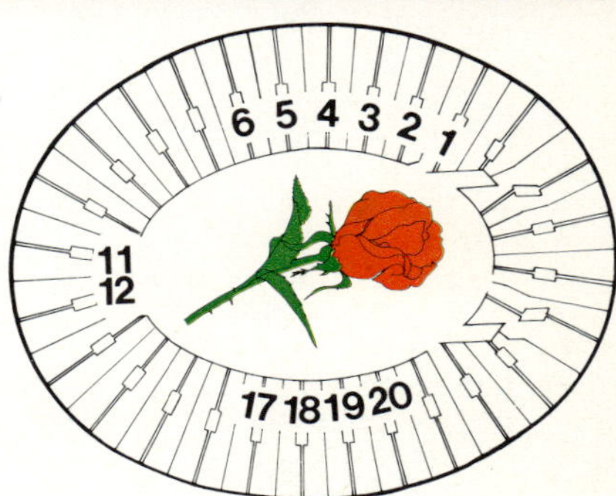

The Rose Bowl. This 104,700-seat stadium will host AFC and NFC winners in 1983's Super Bowl XVII. Built in 1926, it is the traditional home of the annual Pac Ten-Big Ten finale on New Year's Day—the No. 1 college bowl game.

Gambling: Everyone wants a piece of the action. Horseplaying remains a chuck-it-in mania with Americans—but betting football games is rated even ahead of the nags for volume. Some experts claim that *twice* as much is risked on gridplay as on Thoroughbreds.

More than 16 million football fans lay $5 billion with bookies annually, according to the Commission on Review of National Policy Toward Gambling. Pots, pools, parlays and *beating the spread* are the rage, from $1 office-pool players to $10,000-a-game plungers.

Since it's the windup of the pro season, the *Super Bowl* commands the most action. Authorities estimated that up to **$50 million** is wagered on the SB in each of 2 dozen major cities. And not many gamboleers win 50 per cent of their bets.

Knute Rockne, Notre Dame Coach, 1925 (before an Army game): *"Do you want to be the first Notre Dame team to someday tell your grandchildren that you quit?"*

THE PLAYERS: What they do...

SE: The **split end** is primarily a pass-catching target, but must also block for the ball-carrier against a lineman or linebacker coming from the inside outward.

T: Tackles are the big brutes flanking the interior linemen (guards and center). They make various blocks to open holes for the backs, provide interference on power sweeps and protect the QB on pass plays.

G: Guards are the most agile of offensive linemen. The 2 guards block in *The Pit*, make open-field blocks on linebackers, and lead interference on power sweeps both left and right.

C: The **center** has the tough job of passing the ball to the QB and charging even as he snaps it. While thus occupied, he must still execute all the blocks of a guard or tackle.

TE: The **tight end** is a multi-duty blocker who also runs pass routes and may catch the ball short or long in heavy traffic.

RB: Running backs are quadruple-threat men. They must run the ball through holes with speed and power, block for other backs, fake possession of the ball and act as pass-receivers out of the backfield.

FLB: He is a wide receiver or **flankerback** who must shake loose off the scrimmage line to catch passes and block.

QB: The **quarterback's** 2 main duties are (a) lead the team by setting the offensive strategy, and (b) skillfully execute both ground and air plays. He must be an accurate passer. In the huddle before plays, he calls the formation, the play and the snap count for the centering of the ball.

E: Defensive ends are primary attackers of the QB, with mastery of many *stunt* moves to get past blockers. They must also make tackles on wide sweeps or force the ball-carrier out-of-bounds.

T: Defensive tackles try to fight off the pressure of blocks by men attacking them, quickly decipher the play being run and then move to stop it. They're mobile forts.

LB/MLB: Two **linebackers** plus a **middle linebacker** are the secondary line of defense. Their many duties include tackling any ball-carrier who penetrates the front line, breaking up short and medium passes and, at times, blitzing (gang-rushing the quarterback).

CB: The twin **cornerbacks** are the fastest men out there, charged with covering wide receivers on passes while playing either zone or man-for-man defense. Safeties sometimes help them when the CBs are overrun with receivers.

S: Safeties, the last line of defense, are interception magicians. The **strong safety** is so-called because he's stationed opposite the offense's tight end. A **free safety** is one who lines up on the side of the offense's split end.

(page 12: Denver (sic) Cowboys should read Denver Broncos)

Numbering

If you were crouched in the huddle with, let's say, the San Francisco 49ers or Ohio State Buckeyes, you might hear the quarterback say, "We go with 29 Bravo-Alpha on 2." Meaning that the No.2 running back is to carry the ball into the No.9 hole, or around end. *On 2* means the play begins on the QB's second word.

The signal call is based on numbering the linemen and backs. Although the system varies from team to team, many use odd numbers to the right of the center and even numbers to the center's left, ranging from 2 to 8. Single digits then become multiples of 10, so that in the previous example, 20 designates the player (No. 2 back) and 9 denotes his running pattern. Generally, 20s and 40s designate the halfbacks and 30s are for the fullbacks.

Another example: If the QB calls *33*, it means that the fullback (3—or 30) will hit the No.3 hole, or guard slot. *Bravo-Alpha* designates the line-blocking assignments.